I WILL COME

MYSELF

Experiencing the Risen Christ

I WILL COME
MYSELF

Experiencing the Risen Christ

Father Kevin Scallon CM

VERITAS

First published 2008 by
Queenship Publishing Company.
This edition published in 2009 by
Veritas Publications
7–8 Lower Abbey Street
Dublin 1
Ireland
Email publications@veritas.ie
Website www.veritas.ie

ISBN 978 1 84730 164 2

A catalogue record for this book is available from the
British Library.

Printed in the Republic of Ireland
by SPRINT-print Ltd, Dublin

Veritas books are printed on paper made from the wood
pulp of managed forests. For every tree felled, at least one
tree is planted, thereby renewing natural resources.

This book is dedicated to
Christ the King and to
Mary, Queen of the Holy Rosary.

Icon of Christ the High Priest

In an extraordinary confluence of culture, an icon has been created by Peter Dzyuba based on a stained-glass window by the pre-eminent Irish artist Harry Clarke. This window, a masterpiece of the Celtic Byzantine, is in St Mary's Catholic Church in Cong, Co. Mayo, Ireland. Christ the High Priest is vested in the three garments of the priesthood: the dalmatic, the chausable and the omophor, representing the Holy Trinity. Christ's countenance shines in Harry Clarke's window and in Peter Dzyuba's icon as it does through Fr Kevin Scallon's prayerful reflections in this book.

Father Joseph Bertha, Ph.D.
Byzantine Ruthenian Catholic priest

Cover art: Icon of Christ the High Priest
© Peter Dzyuba, iconographer
Used with permission

Contents

Acknowledgements

A book is never the work of just one person, so I am delighted to acknowledge the help I have received in writing this little volume. My thanks to Sr Briege, for her enthusiastic encouragement and prayers; to Jane, who by now knows the text by heart; and to the incomparable Jackie, for her many gifts and skills, and her amazing patience.

Introduction

It gives me great joy and pleasure to introduce to you the author of *I Will Come Myself,* Fr Kevin Scallon CM. It was thirty-two years ago that I had the blessing of meeting Fr Kevin at All Hallows College in Dublin. It was a meeting that certainly changed my life and deepened my love and appreciation for God's gift of the priesthood and His sacraments. Within this book you will find many inspirational stories of the power of the sacraments.

Fr Kevin and I have worked together since 1985 ministering to priests around the world and conducting parish missions. Both of these ministries are very close to the heart of Fr Kevin and, as a Vincentian priest, he continues this work that St Vincent de Paul had begun.

In speaking about the priesthood, Fr Kevin reminds us that the priesthood is not his priesthood, but the priesthood of Jesus Christ. He gives us many beautiful testimonies and stories that illustrate this in his writings. As you read *I Will Come Myself,* you will learn of Fr Kevin's deep love and concern for his brother priests. I know from listening to him how he has encouraged them to always pray for the gifts of the

Holy Spirit, which are so vital and necessary in the lives of all priests. I have been amazed as we minister to priests at the way the Lord uses Fr Kevin to bring great healing and affirmation and encouragement to them. Many seek his guidance and prayers and have told me how grateful they are for his wisdom and insight.

I remember returning home with Fr Kevin after a very busy schedule abroad, having travelled from the Far East, and walking through an airport, a young priest came running up to us with great excitement. He said, 'Oh, Fr Kevin, I prayed that I would meet you. This is a miracle.' And there in the airport he poured out his heart to Fr Kevin. As I walked away, I knew that the Lord had certainly both heard and answered the prayers of this priest.

This book beautifully celebrates the presence of the Risen Christ. Fr Kevin tells of many personal and amazing experiences both in his own life and in the lives of those to whom he has ministered. As you read *I Will Come Myself*, I know you will enjoy Fr Kevin's delightful Irish fun-loving humour. It is known that laughter is the great tonic for the soul and there is no shortage of tonic when you encounter Fr Kevin in the pages of this book.

Sr Briege McKenna OSC

Prologue

When he went into Capernaum a centurion
came up and pleaded with him, 'Sir,' he
said, 'my servant is lying at home paralysed
and in great pain.' Jesus said to him, 'I will
come myself and cure him.' The centurion
replied, 'Sir, I am not worthy to have you
under my roof; just give the word and my
servant will be cured.'

(Matthew 8:5-8)

For such is the power of great minds, such
the lights of truly believing souls, that they
put unhesitating faith in what is not seen
with the bodily eye; they fix their desires on
what is beyond sight. Such fidelity could
never be born in our hearts, nor could
anyone be justified by faith, if our salvation
lay only in what was visible.

And so our Redeemer's visible presence
has passed into the sacraments. Our faith is
nobler and stronger because sight has been
replaced by a truth whose authority is

accepted by believing hearts enlightened from on high. Throughout the world women no less than men, tender girls as well as boys, have given their life's blood in the struggle for this faith. It is a faith that has driven out devils, healed the sick and raised the dead.

(Sermon by St Leo the Great)

I Will Come Myself

Chapter 1
Hearing the Call of God

Vocation in life is something of a mystery. Everyone has a calling in life and each calling has a special value in the sight of God. The most brilliant surgeon is not more important to God than the garbage man; the lawyer is not before the truck driver.

When I was a young boy, I wanted to become many things, depending on my enthusiasm at the moment. In my parish of the Sacred Heart in Irvinestown, County Fermanagh, Northern Ireland, we had an old priest who loved the Lord. His assistant was a younger, quiet man who spent hours in the church praying before the Blessed Sacrament. So from my earliest days I had Godly men who were great role models of the priesthood. It was around the time of my First Communion that I first thought I might like to become a priest.

Ray McAnally was a great Irish actor who played the role of the Cardinal in the movie *The Mission*. In his early years he had gone to the seminary to study for the priesthood. I once heard him being interviewed on the radio and he was asked what he thought a vocation was. He gave what I consider to be a very good description of vocation. He said, 'A vocation is where you begin to suspect that you are about to be called.'

My father and mother loved priests and befriended and supported them. There were always priests coming into our home as far back as I can remember. My earliest memory was that of a chaplain from the US Army during World War II coming for dinner at our home. I remember looking at him and thinking that he did not look at all Irish with his black hair, tanned skin and rimless glasses. There were not many tanned people around my home town in those days and there was no one who wore rimless glasses.

In my teenage years, most secondary schools in Ireland were boarding schools. I went as a boarder to St Patrick's High School in Armagh. St Patrick's was run by the Vincentian Fathers, a community founded by St Vincent de Paul. Going to this school was a very great grace in my life. I had good teachers, but more than that, the priests really impressed me as men who loved the priesthood. They always talked about faith and about Jesus Christ, even in classes not directly about religion.

An important moment for me, relating to my vocation, was going to Confession to one of these Vincentian priests. His name was Fr Hugh. When I went to Fr Hugh, I thought I was talking to Jesus Himself. I know now, of course, that I *was* talking to Jesus, who through the ministry of Fr Hugh revealed Himself to me. It was one of the first experiences of grace that changed me. In Fr Hugh, I had met Jesus – the forgiving, loving and merciful Christ. This priest had certainly acted *in persona Christi*.

Another such moment happened in my senior year in secondary school. One day, walking along the street I saw an old homeless man searching through some rubbish.

I Will Come Myself

Just as I was passing, he turned around and stared at me through his poor, gentle eyes. I don't know why, but at that moment I felt something happen within me and I knew that somehow I had encountered Jesus Christ. When things like this happen, it is hard to describe what it does to you. First, you are not really sure what has happened, and anyway, it is difficult to share it or identify it. The importance of such moments of grace is not in words; it is experienced in the soul, the dwelling place of the Holy Trinity.

It was only later that the Holy Spirit helped me to understand and enabled me to respond to these graces. Unfortunately, people are often told to ignore such graces. They are warned that God does not speak to people. Experiencing God in this way carries with it its own profound conviction. I had experienced God; I just knew it. It changed my life. To say this can't happen is to deny the very words of Jesus and the action of the Holy Spirit: 'He will teach you all things' (John 14:26). These moments of grace are given to many people. It is God who places the consciousness of a vocation into a person's heart and keeps it there. This is what happened to me. I liked the Vincentians, so I became one and have never regretted it. It is important to learn how to listen with the ears of the heart.

Years later, in the summer of 1968, I went to study at the Catholic University of America to get up to speed with the theology of the Second Vatican Council. Many of us priests who were ordained before the council had to do that in order not to be left behind theologically. At the time, Catholic University was a theological volcano with very many priests and religious abandoning their vocations.

I witnessed much confusion and cynicism about the Church. In the midst of it all, I continued with my daily

Eucharist; my devotion to Mary, the Mother of God; the Rosary; and a prayer life that was far from tranquil.

Then the Lord gave me another one of these moments of grace and illumination. It happened like this. In the summer, Washington, DC is hot and humid, so dry cleaning was a regular chore. One afternoon I went down the street to pick up my things from the cleaners. I was dressed for the heat in sandals, T-shirt and shorts. The woman who served me, judging by her accent, was from the Caribbean. When she gave me my change, she looked hard at me and said, 'Are you a priest?'

I said, 'Yes, how did you know?'

She stared at me for a moment and said, 'Because you have the mark of Jesus Christ upon you.'

That 'mark of Jesus Christ' she referred to is the character, that permanent indelible spiritual imprint of the Sacrament of Priesthood. It is the very presence of Christ Himself. It is a unique grace that makes the priest 'another Christ'. If a priest is seeking Christ in prayer, he will begin to desire this transformation. This desire in turn will transform his life and ministry. The more he grows into union with Jesus, the more he will experience the disintegration of his ego and put on the gentleness and humility of Jesus Christ. When the Heavenly Father looks at the priest He sees this mark, this sacramental character in his soul; He sees the image of Jesus, the Jesus of the paschal mystery of our salvation.

Moments such as these are pearls of great price. Jesus can speak to you in a Caribbean accent in order to keep you standing on rock. It was as if He had said, 'Do not forget what you are. Do not forget that I have called you. Do not forget that I am with you. All those around you may forget and walk away, but you must never forget.'

I Will Come Myself

Years after I was ordained a priest, my mother told me that when I was a small boy the parish priest had called to our home to see her. When he was leaving, he gave her a blessing and, pointing to me, said to her, 'This boy will be a priest one day.'

'I never told you this because I wanted you to be what God had planned for you,' she told me. That too was another assurance from God. I thank the Lord that in all my years as a priest I never once doubted the authenticity of my vocation.

I have been working with Sr Briege McKenna for many years. Sr Briege is an Irish Sister of St Clare who is best known throughout the world for her gift of healing. She describes in her extraordinary book *Miracles Do Happen* how the Lord first healed her of crippling arthritis and endowed her with this charism.

'I give you My gift of healing. Go now and use it,' was what He said to her.

Over the years I have seen the Lord perform many miracles through Sr Briege's prayers and her ministry. Even people who listen to her recorded prayers over the telephone or internet have experienced healing. How often have I given praise and thanks to our Lord Jesus Christ for reaching out and touching His suffering people through Sr Briege's prayers.

Not long ago Sr Briege and I went to conduct a priests' retreat in Lithuania where the Church was persecuted and the priests suffered greatly under the Communist regime. They were without their own bishops for several decades. Thankfully, since the fall of the old atheistic government, they now have their own bishops and a brand new seminary which is producing crops of fine young priests. One of the seminarians came to talk to me about his studies. During our conversation he said, 'Would you like me to tell you how I got my vocation?'

I love vocation stories, so I said, 'Sure, I'd love to hear it.' He told me a remarkable story of how the Lord called him to the priesthood.

When he finished I said, 'Would you like to write this down so that I may share it with others?' He agreed. This is what he wrote:

> I am a 33-year-old deacon from Vilnius (Lithuania). In 2000 – a milestone in my life – I had just finished my Bachelor's degree at the Music Academy of Lithuania and had been accepted to study Opera in a Master's program. I felt very content, because there was plenty of work. For example, I produced different entertainment shows, was a master of ceremonies, as well as a singer and drama teacher. During this time, there was no lack of money or women either.
>
> On 15 September that year, I participated in my friend's wedding. The beautiful voice of the priest made the wedding ceremony a glorious event. In the middle of the ceremony I heard someone call me by name. I turned around, but couldn't see anybody. I thought to myself that I had just overheard something and continued to watch the wedding. Then I heard it again: 'Povilas, Povilas!' I turned around, but again I could see nobody calling me. I looked at the people standing beside me, but they didn't look as if they had heard anything. The situation seemed strange to me, but I didn't pay much

attention to it. When I heard somebody calling my name for the third time, I somehow knew that it was God's voice. He told me, 'Your life belongs to Me.'

I soon forgot about this event, but two weeks later He spoke to me again. Just as the first time, I heard His voice not in my head or heart, but audibly, just as I can hear different noises like wind blowing or people talking. God reminded me that my life belongs to Him and showed me the direction I was to take in my life. Even though I was talking to God, I didn't want to agree with His plan as I felt content with my life and didn't have any desire to change it. God didn't argue with me. He just reminded me again that my life belonged to Him.

A conversation like that reoccurred a couple more times during the next two weeks, but I wasn't about to give in. During that year the quality of my singing was rapidly improving and there was hope to make a successful career as a singer. However, at the end of November I started having problems with my voice, and singing became more and more difficult. On the eve of each concert I sang in, the Lord would ask me to answer His calling. I would promise to think about His plan if He healed my voice for the next day's performance. The next day after the successful performance I would rudely tell God that I didn't want to hear about His calling. The sickness would then come back.

I am ashamed now to admit that during that year my behaviour toward God was obnoxious. In fact, I was ruder than I have been with anybody else before – even compared to those who wished me ill. I continued being rude and kept trying His patience until 12 January, a day before a special concert given in memory of the events that occurred on 13 January in 1991 (the USSR army attacked the Republic of Lithuania). I was invited to sing live on national television. That morning during the rehearsal I completely lost my voice. My doctor refused to continue treatment admitting that she couldn't detect the source of my sickness and that my body wasn't reacting to any medication.

The next two weeks were the hardest in my life. I felt as though I had lost the foundation of my life. I was crying out to God, but He was silent. Finally I understood that God used this situation to talk to me as a way of getting my attention.

Then I promised God that if He gave me my voice back, I would seriously consider His plan; however, if I decided not to follow it, He would stop pursuing me. His agreement to this pact was the last time that I audibly heard God's voice. While fulfilling my promise to God, I started seriously considering becoming a priest. At the same time I was secretly hoping that I would conclude that this was not my calling. Then I started reading the Bible, which I hadn't done before. I was shocked to read about the callings of both the prophet Samuel and the apostle Paul. In some ways these were similar to mine. Because of these similarities, for three years I was embarrassed to tell my story to anybody except my parents.

At the end of January 2001, almost a year later, I woke up one day with the knowledge in my heart that God had changed my heart and that His calling had become the way of my life. I immediately shared this with my parents and my girlfriend whom I then loved.

I thought that I was happy before God called me to Himself. But I never even imagined that it is possible to be so happy when you place your life in the hands of God.

Sometimes people who have heard my story ask me why God chose such an unusual way to communicate with me. While praying about it I understood that it wasn't because I was better than others, but simply because I was 'deaf' to all of His other invitations. God used what it took to draw my attention and to help me hear His voice when I was 'deaf'.

Thank You, Lord, for Your calling and thank You for Your unlimited love and patience with Your once 'deaf' child.

I know another priest who was raised by his parents to be a Communist. He studied in Russia and trained to become a subversive back in his own country. Eventually he returned home and began to work for the Communist Party. He did not believe in God. One day, when he was lying on a beach somewhere in the Mediterranean with his girlfriend, he heard an inner voice say to him, 'Get up. Go home. I want you to become a priest.'

He told me, 'I hardly knew what a priest was.'

In any event, he did what he was told and became a priest. Those who insist that priestly vocations come solely from the local Church community need to take account of experiences like these. Jesus continues to call men just as He did in the Gospel when He called the disciples and when He called St Paul on the road to Damascus. The history of the Church is full of examples of people who were called in this way and were given the grace of vocation to the priesthood.

Chapter 2
You Are Jesus Christ

The last period of my short missionary career was spent in Biafra, a breakaway province of Nigeria, and the cause of a civil war in that country. I was the pastor at a parish where there was a great number of local people and an equal number of refugees. I was the only priest in the parish, with responsibility for this great multitude of poor, hungry people. They were literally starving because of the long blockade that destroyed the economy and prevented the normal flow of food supplies to their towns and villages.

At the time, I was both priest and farmer, as well as motor mechanic and generally responsible for the well-being of so many people. Part of my task was to divide the meager supplies of relief foods and medicine that were flown in every night and distributed to the parishes to be given to the people. I did not have the faith in those days to pray for the multiplication of the loaves and fishes, not believing that it would happen. But I did what I could.

Every morning when I would rise, my compound would be filled with poor, starving women and children. It was heartbreaking to look at them. On Sundays I would travel around the parish celebrating Mass in different places and telling people to be sure to plant crops themselves and not to rely too much on the relief supplies.

One morning after returning from celebrating two or three Masses, I arrived back at my mission to discover that there was no one waiting for me. I thanked God for this respite, but just as I was walking through the door of the mission, a frail young woman came around the corner of the house.

'Good morning, Father,' she said to me.

At that moment my mind was on my breakfast of instant coffee, boiled eggs and toast. I didn't greet her, but said to her rather gruffly, 'What do you want?'

Again, she said, 'Good morning, Father.'

And I said, 'Good morning' to her. Nothing happens in Africa until you have said 'Good morning'.

She then said, 'Father, can I tell you my story?'

Still thinking of my breakfast, I groaned inwardly at the thought of having to listen to another sad story. However, knowing that I would have to listen to her one way or another, I said, 'Yes, please tell me your story.'

She told me that she was from a place about sixty kilometers south of where we were. She recounted a terrible tale of how she was forced from her home by the soldiers and how her husband and her three children had all died of starvation and hepatitis. I had little difficulty believing her because at the time so many were dying of hepatitis and malnutrition. The wonder was that we didn't all die of this terrible

I Will Come Myself

disease. When she had finished, she said, 'Father, please give me something to keep my body and soul together until this time passes.'

I instructed the catechist to bring her some food and clothing and other bits and pieces that she obviously needed. When she received each of these items she placed them on the ground in front of where I was standing and began to sing and to dance around them. Still thinking of my breakfast, I said to the catechist, 'What is she singing about?'

He said, 'Father, she is thanking God for you.'

'Really?' I said. At the mention of God I decided that I should try to evangelise this poor lost soul. I said to her, 'So you believe in God then, do you?'

She gave me a look of disbelief and said, 'Of course I believe in God.'

I think she had it on the tip of her tongue to ask me whether I believed in God or not, but charitably she did not.

I then said to her, 'And do you believe in Jesus Christ?'

To this question she made no reply, but went and picked up from the ground the food, clothing and other things that had been given to her. She then came over and stood directly in front of me and said, 'Father, you are asking me whether I believe in Jesus Christ. For me, today, you are Jesus Christ.'

I believe that God sends us angels to help us at special moments in our lives. Perhaps on that Sunday morning I had forgotten what I had gone there to do. Maybe I was becoming more of a social worker and relief officer than a priest. In those days, I was so busy serving others that I had little time to think of my own need for God. I was young. I was healthy and full of energy, and felt that I could do everything by myself. So I believe that God sent me this special messenger to remind me of what was important in my life.

On that hot Sunday morning, this poor frail woman, in one short sentence, gave me the best definition that I have ever heard of what it means to be a priest. A priest is a man who makes Jesus Christ present.

Her words, 'Today, for me, you are Jesus Christ', were straight from the Holy Spirit. Her description of what it means to be a priest was such a grace-filled moment and made such an impression on me that I have never forgotten it. Her words have been a kind of theological shorthand reminding me of my priestly identity.

In the past, the words *alter Christus*, which mean 'another Christ', were used as a description of priestly identity. It was a perfect description of priesthood. Since the Second Vatican Council, the priest is described as one who acts *in persona Christi capitis* – in the person of Christ, the head of His Body, the Church. This, too, is a beautiful and apt description of the priesthood. I have often told the story of this woman. Her memory remains still fresh in my mind and her words still echo in my heart. As a priest, whether I am aware of it or not, I am called to be the very presence of Jesus Christ to everyone. I know that I should never act or speak in a way that would embarrass Jesus. I am a priest not just when I am on the altar or hearing Confessions or anointing the sick. I am always a priest. At a ball game or the theatre, at a parish meeting or at a Church conference, I am called to be the very presence of Christ; and as St Paul says, 'the sweet fragrance of Jesus Christ'.

Chapter 3
Emmanuel the Apostle

In that same hour he rejoiced in the Holy
Spirit and said, 'I thank thee, Father, Lord
of heaven and earth, that thou hast hidden
these things from the wise and
understanding and revealed them to
babes.'

(Luke 10:21)

I arrived in my old Volkswagen, having driven over
dusty clay Nigerian roads dotted with plenty of
potholes, enough to make you seasick. The village
elders met me and welcomed me and showed me into
the mud house that would be my home for the next
few weeks. Tired and hungry, I was anxious to rest for
a while.

Just as I had begun to settle into my new
surroundings, there was a knock on the door. It was a
frail-looking boy of about eleven or twelve years. 'Are
you the mission priest?' he asked.

'Yes,' I said. 'What is it you want?'

'My name is Emmanuel. I have come to help you
with the mission.'

'And how are you going to help me, Emmanuel?' I asked.

'My father is the parish catechist,' he said, 'and I know all the catechism. You can ask me any question you like and I will answer it. And I know all the prayers too. He handed me an old battered catechism.

'Go ahead and ask me anything and see for yourself. I know it all.'

He was as good as his word. He knew it inside out, prayers and all. He even knew prayers I didn't know myself. 'So,' I said, looking at this strange little Nigerian boy, 'How do you plan to help me?'

He replied, 'This is a very big village, Father, and there are many children here who have never been baptised, and more who need to prepare for First Communion and Confirmation. I will teach them the catechism and get them ready. I will teach three classes each day – one for Baptism, one for First Confession and Communion, and one for Confirmation. I will teach one early in the morning, one before mid-day and one later in the afternoon. When I have finished, Father, you can examine them and see how they do.'

I said. 'I will have to talk to your father first'. His father Cyril, who loved his little boy, assured me that Emmanuel was equal to the task.

So the mission began and I was busy with many things. Day by day, coming and going, I would see Emmanuel with his flock around him, teaching them the catechism and the prayers. Little Emmanuel would not have used the term Sacrament of Initiation. That would come later with the new liturgy of the Second Vatican Council. But he would have known that Baptism, Confirmation and the Eucharist were essential to becoming a member of the Church. These sacraments prepare us and make us members of the Body of Christ, the Church, and enable us to become mature members of Christ.

One of Emmanuel's pupils stopped me one day on the road and said, 'Emmanuel says that when I am baptised I will become a child of God. Is that true?'

'It is true,' I said. 'Are you preparing for Baptism?'

'Yes,' he said. 'I want to become a child of God.'

When I heard the boy say this, I asked myself what it was that put such thoughts and desires into his heart. Where does such a desire come from? Surely it is the work of the Holy Spirit. How easy it is to evangelise children; how simply they embrace the idea of God and religion.

Meanwhile, back under the palm trees, Emmanuel continued to work with his tattered little catechism, doing what Jesus told the apostles, 'Go therefore and make disciples of all nations, baptising them in the name of the Father, and of the Son and of the Holy Spirit, teaching them to observe all that I have commanded you; and lo, I am with you always, to the close of the age' (Matthew 28:19-20).

Each morning of this prolonged parish mission when I went to pray, no matter how early I went, Emmanuel would be there before me. He would come in and go up and kneel on the floor in front of the tabernacle with his hands folded in prayer. I used to wonder what would make a young boy act in this way. To most, such behaviour would appear unusual, even peculiar. But there is nothing unusual about it. Emmanuel was a little boy who had clearly experienced the presence of Jesus in the tabernacle and had come to know Christ in a deeply personal and mystical way. He no longer needed to believe that Jesus was present in the Blessed Sacrament; he knew that He was there.

In one of his first homilies as Pope, Benedict XVI said: 'And only when God is seen does life truly begin. Only when we meet the living God in Christ do we know what life is ... There is nothing more beautiful than to be surprised by the Gospel, by this encounter with Jesus Christ. There is nothing more beautiful than to know Him and to speak to others of our friendship with Him.'

As I looked at this saintly, prayerful boy, I found myself filled with admiration and a kind of holy envy. Clearly he had a deeper, richer and more intimate relationship with Jesus Christ than I had. Without a doubt, Emmanuel had encountered the living Christ in the sacraments.

There is simply nothing more beautiful. This pious child had experienced Jesus and delighted in telling others about Him. Emmanuel was a perfect example of what the Catechism of the Catholic Church speaks of when it says:

> The transmission of the Christian faith consists primarily in proclaiming Jesus Christ in order to lead others to faith in him. From the beginning, the first disciples burned with the desire to proclaim Christ: 'We cannot but speak of what we have seen and heard'.
>
> (*CCC:* 425)

Near the end of the mission, Emmanuel came to me and said, 'Father, all my students are ready. Would you please examine them?'

This was arranged with the catechist and some teachers and we held an oral examination of all Emmanuel's students. It was exactly as he promised. They knew all the catechism answers and they had a good understanding of what the answers meant. The following Saturday was to be the Baptism of Emmanuel's pupils. Sunday was to be the First Communion Mass. Emmanuel was dressed very poorly. He had no shoes and his T-shirt and pants had seen better days. As a gift to him I sent him with his mother to get some new clothes for his big weekend. He came back with a new shirt, new trousers and new sandals.

On Sunday before Mass I looked for Emmanuel and saw him still dressed in his old clothes. After Mass I asked him what had happened to his new outfit.

He said, 'Father, please do not be angry with me and let me explain.'

I said, 'How could I be angry with you, Emmanuel. Did you give them away?'

'Let me tell you what happened,' he said. 'You remember in one of your sermons you talked about St Martin, when he was a soldier, he gave half his cloak to a beggar standing in the snow and that night in a dream Christ appeared to St Martin wearing his cloak.'

'Well,' he said, 'on Saturday when I was returning to my village, I met a boy and he was crying. I asked him "Why are you crying?" He told me that he was to make his First Communion on Sunday and he had no decent clothes to wear.'

I said, 'Don't tell me what you did, Emmanuel.'

'Yes, Father,' he said. 'What else could I do? I said to the boy, "Take these new clothes. They are for you."'

He pointed and said, 'Look at him, Father, there he is over there.' And sure enough, a few yards away, there he was dressed in Emmanuel's new shirt and pants and sandals. I was so moved I could hardly speak.

The following Monday, after many speeches by parishioners and their generous giving of gifts, I got ready to leave. I looked around to see if I could find Emmanuel in the crowd. He was not standing at the front with his father and mother and the head men of the village. He was hidden in the back behind some other boys, waving as I drove off.

Some months later I received a letter from the priest at that mission. He wrote, 'You remember your friend Emmanuel. I am writing to tell you that he became ill some weeks ago. We took him to the hospital and the sisters quickly diagnosed that he was suffering tuberculosis. In spite of all their efforts, they could not save him and he died peacefully after receiving Holy Communion. When I last visited him, he said to me, "When I go to heaven, write to Fr Kevin and ask him to offer Mass for me."'

God has a destiny for all His children. Parents can foster and promote this destiny or they can frustrate it or prevent it. Either way, it will not go unnoticed by God. Why is the memory of this boy Emmanuel so fresh to me? Why did his spirit make such an impact on my spirit? It is because he made Christ present and real to me and to those He taught. Jesus lived in Emmanuel; He spoke through him and taught through him. Christ was in him; he was Christ to all of us. I pray that he will be as much help to me as I approach the last phase of my priestly ministry as he was at the beginning. Jesus comes to us in many forms, even as a frail African boy.

Little Emmanuel was a saint, an innocent pure soul who was loved by Jesus Christ, who drew him more and more into His Eucharistic Presence and drew others into that same presence through him. His child's heart was united to Christ's heart which enabled him to care for others. He was never ashamed to share his piety and faith.

I have never met any child who did not instantly believe in God, in Jesus, in prayer, in the presence of Jesus in the Blessed Sacrament, in Mary, and in the difference between good and evil and all that is in the Gospels. That is why it is so important for parents to pay great attention to teaching their children the faith and forming them in ways of holiness.

Today, unfortunately, many parents neglect to do this. They leave their children to fend for themselves. Parents who knowingly refuse to hand on the faith to their children will be held accountable for their neglect.

Chapter 4
You and Me

In the fall of 1972, I found myself in San Francisco while en route to Sydney, Australia, where I was to conduct two retreats. I had taken the bus from the airport to the downtown depot. I decided to go into a diner for a cup of coffee. After a few minutes, a man came over to me and said, 'Hi, Father! I guess you're here for the Full Gospel Business Men's Convention.'

'I'm sorry?' I said.

'The Full Gospel Business Men,' he said. 'They are having their convention in the Hilton Hotel just down the street.'

I thought to myself, whatever this strange-sounding meeting is, I am definitely not going to it. I replied, 'Actually no, I have no plans for that.'

He said, 'You'll meet a lot of Catholics there and there'll be priests there too.'

I thanked him and he left. A few minutes later, another man came over and we had much the same conversation. Again, I politely declined and he went away. Then a woman came with the same invitation, telling me how much I would enjoy it. So after some thought, I said to myself, 'What harm could it do? I am hardly going to lose my faith.'

So I went down the street to the Hilton Hotel. The girl at the desk told me where the convention hall was and I took the lift up to the third floor. I went into this huge auditorium, obviously at a break. People started coming up to me and when they heard I was from Ireland, they hugged me and shook my hand as though I was the Prodigal Son. When the music ministry started up, I stood with everyone else and sang *How Great Thou Art*. I was very taken by the whole atmosphere of the singing and the prayer and the praise. People started sharing about what God was doing in their lives. After listening for sometime, I began to feel uneasy and said to myself, 'This is no place for a respectable seminary priest from Ireland.' So I left quietly, thinking no one would notice.

I went down the stairs into the hotel lobby. As I was crossing to the door, this huge man dressed in western garb complete with boots, hat, belt, string tie and shirt walked up to me. He took me by the hand and shook it warmly and proceeded to give me a bear hug. He said, 'Gee, Father, it's real good to see you. You are the first Catholic priest I have met since I got here. You sure are welcome.'

Then he said, 'My name is George and I'm from Texas.'

I was about to say, 'I would never have guessed,' but I reckoned that at that moment repartee would have been out of place.

He then beckoned with his hand and about five other equally tall men dressed in the same western style appeared, it seemed, out of nowhere. They all

I Will Come Myself

shook my hand and gave me rib-cracking, manly hugs. We talked politely for a few moments. For some reason while all this was going on, I was getting madder and madder. I'm not sure why I was so angry, but I suppose it was because these good men were embarrassing me. Anyway, that's how I felt. I remember thinking, I hope no one from Ireland who knows me, passes by at this moment or my reputation will be in tatters.

Then the leader said, 'Father, why don't you lead us in prayer for God's blessing on our convention?'

I felt completely trapped. I had never led anyone in a spontaneous prayer in my life. In desperation I suggested that we pray 'the prayer that Jesus taught us to say to our Heavenly Father'. There we stood, several large Texans and me holding hands in the middle of the lobby of the Hilton Hotel in San Francisco on a Saturday afternoon while I was getting angrier by the minute. I almost shook myself free of them and made a charge for the door. Did I hear the Lord saying, 'You like John Wayne? I'll give you all the John Waynes you want.' As I burst through the door, I ran into a Hare Krishna man ringing his bells and beating his drum, and I almost sent him flying.

Outside, I walked down the street away from the hotel feeling really upset. As I walked, the words of Jesus to Nicodemus dropped into my mind, 'Are you a master in Israel and you do not know these things'? (John 3:10). These words pierced me as though Jesus had spoken them to me personally. For there I was, a 'Master in Israel', a respectable seminary priest, having to be led unwillingly in prayer by a group of strange men who were a lot more free in the Spirit than I was and who obviously had a more intimate relationship with Jesus than I had.

I felt humbled and ashamed, but in a strange way, also grateful to God. Looking back now I see that this was another one of those precious moments of grace. And were these men from Texas or were they angels? Or was the Lord having a little joke at my expense, knowing my love for all things western? 'Master in Israel?' Not hardly.

For most of the 1970s I was on the faculty at All Hallows Seminary in Dublin. All of our seminarians were ordained to serve in dioceses outside of Ireland, many of them in the United States. One summer I decided to go and work in a diocese in New Mexico where some of our alumni were destined to serve after their ordination. I found myself the acting pastor in the town of Winslow, Arizona, right on the famous Route 66. Part of my ministry, I discovered, was to receive and check the hats and boots of local people who came into town on Fridays to receive their welfare checks. They were all men who spent the weekend savouring the delights of a variety of beverages, not all of them health-giving. They would come back on Monday morning in differing stages of fragility, at which time I would reunite them with their hats and boots. I'm not sure which of the Beatitudes it applies to, but perhaps *Blessed are the boot-keepers, their soles will be saved.*

In my rectory there were two young priests from Mexico who were there to learn English. Our cook was a Mexican lady who had a great love for chilli, salsa and every kind of Mexican food. During my time there I tasted a great variety of her excellent cooking, but I never once saw a potato. It's not that I didn't like

Mexican food; it's just that, well, you really can have too much of a good thing.

The older of the two priests persuaded me to accompany him to the local prayer meeting. He neglected to tell me that it was in Spanish. Afterwards, I said to myself, 'Never again.'

This was my first experience of a Charismatic prayer meeting and only strengthened my resolve to avoid anything connected with the Charismatic Renewal. At the time, it did not sit well with my traditional Irish Catholic upbringing.

As the summer drew on, my frustration deepened. So I was glad to pack my bags and head back to Ireland, the land of the potato, fresh milk, brown bread and meat that was not disguised by sour green and white substances quite alien to the Celtic palate. On my way home I had arranged with an alumnus of All Hallows to stay a day or two in his parish of St Catherine of Siena in Phoenix, Arizona. It had not been a great summer for me and by now my mood was grey, to say the least.

On my first morning at St Catherine's I arose and had my breakfast, went for a walk, and then decided to 'say a few prayers'. The rectory had a little chapel and I went in to spend some time in prayer. I began with the Morning Prayer of the Church from the Divine Office and, having finished this, I closed the book and put it aside. I sat there, my mind a complete blank, unhappy about the last few weeks in Winslow. After about six or seven minutes, something happened that changed my entire life. As I sat there distractedly looking at the door of the tabernacle, I suddenly saw Jesus. I was aware that even though it appeared to be an external vision, it was actually internal. He was smiling and laughing at me. It was a friendly, loving laughter; not one of ridicule or anything like that.

I said to Him, 'Why are You laughing at me?'

'Because,' He said, 'You are always complaining.'

This reply struck me: firstly, because it was devoid of any negative or critical content; and secondly, because it was so true. I have always believed that the Lord allows us to experience interior spiritual crises from time to time in order to get us to move from where we are to where He wants us to be. My crisis was not connected with my priestly calling; thank God I have never had any doubt about that. It was just a sense of dissatisfaction with myself, that somehow there should be more to my relationship with God and my priestly ministry than I was experiencing.

So when Jesus said, 'Because you are always complaining,' I knew exactly what He meant.

This amazing dialogue seemed nevertheless normal and spontaneous, and so I replied, 'Well, if You felt the way I feel, You would complain too.'

Then the Lord gave me a look of intense love and said very seriously, 'But don't you know that all that matters is you and Me?'

That was the end of my very first mystical experience. It all seemed to be so natural, and yet it changed my life completely. It was what Pope John Paul II called a 'personal encounter with the risen Christ'.

My first reaction to this experience was one of disbelief and denial. I said to myself, 'Things are worse than I thought. Not only am I hearing voices, but I'm starting to see things as well.' Mental health people will tell you these are not good symptoms.

I Will Come Myself

When I returned to Ireland I shared what had happened with holy people whom I trusted and they confirmed what I already knew in my heart, that the Lord had spoken to me.

In prayer a day or so later, that inner voice of Christ spoke to me again and said, 'Are you now going to take our relationship more seriously by a new life of prayer?' So my prayer life became very much deeper. My celebration of the Liturgy of the Divine Office was different, the Scriptures exploded into new life for me, my Confessions and my celebration of the Eucharist were transformed, and my experience of being a priest changed forever. My suspicion and opposition to the Charismatic Renewal movement dissolved and I felt a strong conviction that the Lord wanted me to bring this renewal to the priesthood, which eventually led me to begin the *Intercession for Priests* at All Hallows Seminary.

Chapter 5
Intercession for Priests

The greatest crisis to hit the Catholic Church since the Second Vatican Council involved the Catholic priesthood. It is a crisis which continues to this day in one form or another. While at All Hallows Seminary, a period of Copernican change took place when tried and true methods of priestly formation were abandoned in favour of academic and personal freedoms, which have inflicted a wound on the Church.

In our seminary we were hearing of alumni leaving the ministry, usually to get married; some after decades in the priesthood, some after just a few years. My doubt about the wisdom of their decision remains with me to this day and I feel sure that with timely help, many would have weathered the storm and remained true to their priestly promises. One former priest told me that he went to his Provincial Superior to complain about his impossibly heavy workload and said that he was thinking of leaving the priesthood. Without any attempt to speak to him, counsel him or even listen, the Superior said that he would try to arrange the priest's departure as quickly as possible. He said, 'If my

Superior had taken just a little time to speak to me and listen to my situation, I am sure I would still be a priest today. I know I would.' These departures began as a trickle, but soon became a great stream leaving the pastoral ministry of the Church severely depleted. A similar exodus from religious communities was taking place at the same time.

No one really knew what to do about this crisis in the priesthood and in the seminaries. The response by the authorities in most seminaries was to yield to student demands, which was clearly not the answer.

It was almost by accident, on a visit to the United States in 1975, that I came across a movement started by Fr George Kosicki called the *Intercession for Priests*. The idea for the *Intercession* was to invite priests to come together, to pray and intercede for the spiritual and personal renewal of priests. Having taken part in it for a week, the idea of starting it in Ireland took root in my mind. The following summer of 1976, I decided to start it in All Hallows College. It was scheduled to begin on 16 July, the Feast of Our Lady of Mount Carmel. Two days before, only one priest had registered. I talked to my Superior and told him my dilemma. He said, 'Don't worry, let us see what happens.' I talked to an Auxiliary Bishop of Dublin, Bishop Dermot O'Mahoney, who gave me what I now see was a real direction from the Holy Spirit. He said, 'Even if there are only two of you, begin.'

On that opening day, 16 July, another providential happening took place in the person of Sr Briege McKenna. I had been asked if I would like to meet Sr Briege, who was in Ireland at the time. I had many things to concern me that day, but I agreed and she arrived on a Saturday afternoon. Sr Briege to that point had spent most of her religious life teaching at St Lawrence Catholic School in Tampa, Florida. She was becoming well known for her gift of healing and miracles throughout the United States and Ireland. She had heard about the *Intercession* and was anxious to meet me, as she herself was beginning to become involved in working for priests. She had already travelled to South America to give retreats to clergy. It quickly became evident to me that in addition to her gift of healing, Sr Briege had also a distinct charism of ministry to priests. She had great love for the Church and a great respect and regard for the priesthood. Little knowing what lay ahead, I asked Sr Briege if she would like to pray with the priests. She agreed and in due course became a permanent member of the core group. She has not once failed to attend the *Intercession*, bringing her unique ministry to thousands of priests. In 1985, Sr Briege and I, with the blessing of our respective Superiors, were sent out to expand the ministry to priests literally to the ends of the earth.

And so, on 16 July 1976, the *Intercession for Priests* began quite symbolically with twelve priests and still continues each year during the month of August for over thirty-two years.

Here are some comments from over the years of priests who have attended the *Intercession*:

> It has always been of great help for me to attend the *Intercession for Priests*. It really can only be understood by experience.

No one can describe how it happens, but it is a spiritual experience beyond words which helps me to appreciate my priesthood more and more. Thank you for having started and for continuing with *Intercession for Priests.*

Since we cannot have re-ordination, the good Lord has given us the *Intercession for Priests.*

And my good friend and colleague, Monsignor Terence Stonehill, said:

Any priest who wishes to be renewed spiritually and to experience a deeper gift of prayer and love for the Eucharist, who wishes to fan the flame of holiness in his priesthood, to experience the outpouring of the gifts of the Holy Spirit, should come to the *Intercession for Priests.*

Chapter 6
Jesus the Housecleaner

An Irish priest who had attended the *Intercession for Priests* invited me to give three priests' retreats in the country where he was working as a missionary. It was not long after my own personal encounter with the Risen Lord, so I was, as they say, excited and delighted to be going. My audience was composed of expatriate missionaries from all over Europe and North America. During the first retreat I very quickly realised that none of the priests shared anything of my new-found enthusiasm and were, to put it mildly, not impressed. So the retreat went badly.

The second retreat, held in a different part of the country was, if possible, worse than the first. So by the time it came to conduct the third retreat, my morale was low. In any case, I decided to ratchet up my zeal and enthusiasm and make a special effort for these missionary priests.

On the first evening I explained what we were going to do. We would meet and pray the Divine Office, after which we would have a period of singing and spontaneous prayer. So we met and celebrated Morning Prayer, but as for singing and spontaneous prayer – nothing. I myself sang like Pavarotti, but failed to impress. Afterwards, a few of them asked for a meeting with me. They were afraid that I was going to make them sing in tongues and were reassured when I told them I would not. They also commented on the 'faith sharing' groups that were scheduled. They said, 'We don't do that,' which I translated to be, 'We are not going to do that.' Again I reassured them.

Next morning, day two, we met again for Morning Prayer and again, no one sang and no one prayed; or should I say, no one dared to. They sat there, about thirty of them, like a room full of statues, with their arms folded, projecting an air of mystical defiance: *We shall not be moved.* By now, I was really down, but I struggled on manfully and began to give them my first talk of the day. After two minutes into this brilliant presentation, one of them, a small dark-haired Italian priest, raised his hand and said, 'Please may I speak?'

Before I could say, 'No, you may not,' he was on his feet speaking.

He said, 'Excuse me, Father, but what is all this talk about the Holy Spirit?'

This took me by surprise, because I had hardly mentioned the Holy Spirit up to that point.

He continued, 'You know, Father, when we were baptised, we all received the Holy Spirit, didn't we?' and he appealed to the brethren who quietly concurred.

'And then when we were confirmed, we received even more of the Holy Spirit,' and again he appealed to his confreres and got their support.

'And as for what happened when we were ordained, what an abundance of the Holy Spirit did we not receive? But what is this you are talking about? Is this some other Holy Spirit, some new sacrament?'

He said, 'You talk like a commercial for instant coffee, except with you, it's not instant coffee, but instant Holy Spirit. You put some in and stir it up and lo and behold, out comes the Holy Spirit.'

He finished with one of those gestures that only Italians can make, and then sat down. As he did so, the brothers nodded their heads and murmured their sagacious approval.

Obviously, things had not gone too well for me up to this point. Now I was looking disaster in the face. I prayed a prayer of despair, 'Lord, not even You can redeem this retreat.' I hoped that the ground might open up and swallow me. I don't know how I got through the rest of my talk, but somehow I did. After that there was lunch and the merciful siesta. I lay awake in the hot African afternoon, wondering if it would be possible to change my flight and leave the next day, or better yet, that same evening. But the Lord had other plans. Unknown to me, He had decided to *come Himself*.

After siesta, I went to get some strong tea to revive myself before Mass. Walking along the path to the dining room I saw my interrogator of the morning walking toward me. Because of my anger at him, I pretended not to see him. But he ran up to me in a state of agitation. He said, 'Father, I have to speak to you right away.'

I had no idea what to make of this, so I brought him back to my room.

He said, 'Father, I have something to tell you. Please listen to me.'

I Will Come Myself

He told me of an experience he had after the morning talk. When he had finished I said, 'Joseph, do me a favour, would you?'

He said, 'Certainly, Father, anything.'

I said, 'Would you please share with the others at Mass what you just told me?

'Gladly,' he said.

So, at the Eucharist, after my homily, I said to the priests, 'Father Joseph would like to share something with you.' At first they did not know how to react and they looked at Joseph with quiet puzzlement.

He began: 'You remember that I spoke to Father [meaning me] this morning. I was very angry and had made up my mind to leave the retreat. On my way to pick up my things and go home, I was passing the chapel and for some reason I went in. I walked up to the front seat and sat down. I began to shake my fist at the tabernacle and said to Jesus, "Jesus, You are speaking to him out there. Speak to me now."'

He said, 'No sooner were these words out of my mouth, when suddenly I had a vision. It was like watching a movie screen. In this vision I was driving in my pickup truck up to my mission house, admiring the flowers and shrubs and the building which I had designed and constructed with my own hands.'

(I should explain that in every mission territory there is usually a priest or a brother who is in charge of all building and construction. This man will build you anything from a toilet to a cathedral, depending on your need. Father Joseph, being from Italy, was a master builder.)

He continued: 'My vision changed and I found myself inside my house and there were all my possessions in a great pile in the middle of the floor – my clothes, my shoes, my books, etcetera; and there was a man with a gigantic shovel, shovelling everything out through the back door. When I went over to stop him I found myself looking into the face of Jesus, who leaned over and put a finger to my lips and said, 'Joseph, I have come to clean out your house. Go and stand outside.' The vision changed again. Now I found myself standing outside watching all my precious possessions come flying through the air and landing in the yard.

'As I looked on I became aware of a woman coming towards me from my right. I looked around and there was Mary, the Mother of Jesus. I ran over to her and said, "Look what He is doing in my house." She stopped me and said, "Joseph, my son, let Him do what must be done."

'At that moment the bell rang for lunch and my vision ended and to my astonishment I found myself sitting in the front row seat of the chapel overawed at what I had just experienced. I got up and as I was walking down the centre aisle of the chapel, aware that there was no one there except myself, I heard clearly the sound of monks singing a verse from Psalm 95: "If today you hear the voice of the Lord, harden not your hearts."'

With these astonishing words Joseph sat down and the 'eyes of everyone were upon him'. I have heard of people listening open-mouthed, but I had never seen it until that evening. These were the men who did not want faith sharing, but what they got was an unbelievable sharing of one man's faith encounter with the Risen Christ. The effect of Joseph's witness was astonishing, electrifying. Everyone on that retreat was transformed, myself most of all. Here was this little

I Will Come Myself

man, who only hours before was protesting in front of all of us that this kind of thing does not happen, now telling of his own amazing personal encounter with the Risen Lord.

I do not know what Joseph was like before, but after subsequent conversations with him, I can say that the new Joseph was a gentle, self-effacing and humble man. He said to me, 'You know, Fr Kevin, my house really needed to be cleaned out. I tried to do it myself more than once, but I am glad that Jesus came and did it for me.'

My lament of the previous day, that even God could not redeem this retreat, was now a bittersweet taste in my mouth. Jesus did redeem the retreat and in doing so taught me the lesson of a lifetime. May the Lord forgive me for all the times that I let my ego get in His way.

How wonderful it is to be part of these marvellous moments of grace. How merciful the Lord was to a poor, egocentric, frustrated and fairly angry priest who had imagined that he had something to give to these good missionary priests. Jesus said to the Centurion, *'I will come Myself'* (Matthew 8:7). He says the same to all of us who are called to evangelise.

Every follower of Christ, especially priests, must be ready to allow Jesus to act in and through them. There are so many opportunities for us to stand aside and allow Jesus to work.

For years, Joseph would send me a Christmas card. At the bottom he always wrote, 'I still remember our wonderful retreat.' I am sure he did and so do I. I have never again said to the Lord, 'Not even You could redeem this retreat.'

Chapter 7
I Will Come Myself

In Chapter 2 of the First Epistle of Peter we read, 'But you are a chosen race, a royal priesthood, a holy nation, God's own people' (1 Peter 2:9). Every baptised Christian shares in the universal priesthood of Jesus Christ. In living our Baptism each day we exercise this priesthood and as such we are mediators between God and the world, between Christ and His Church. Christ comes into the world and speaks to and dwells among His people through us believers. We are His voice, His hands, His ears. His mercy and forgiveness come to sinners through us.

The priestly ministry, however, is given to certain men whom Jesus calls to serve the Church. This expression of Christ's priesthood is essentially different from the priesthood of the baptised. The ordained priest is entrusted by Jesus with His very own ministry and powers. He is to celebrate the Eucharist and the other sacraments, thereby making the forgiving, healing and sanctifying Christ present to His people. He must prophetically proclaim the Word of God. When he speaks, Christ speaks. When he blesses, Christ blesses and makes holy. The priest must always be in tune with the Holy Spirit.

There is a beautiful prayer in the Byzantine Rite of Ordination that the bishop prays while he is laying hands on those he is ordaining:

> Lord, fill with the gift of the Holy Spirit him whom you have deigned to raise to the rank of the priesthood, that he may be worthy to stand without reproach before your altar, to proclaim the Gospel of your kingdom, to fulfill the ministry of your word of truth, to offer you spiritual gifts and sacrifices, to renew your people by the bath of rebirth; so that he may go out to meet our great God and Saviour Jesus Christ, your only Son, on the day of his second coming, and may receive from your vast goodness the recompense for a faithful administration of his order.
>
> (*CCC*: 1587)

St Gregory of Nazianzus, as a very young priest, wrote:

> We must begin by purifying ourselves before purifying others; we must be instructed to be able to instruct, become light to illuminate, draw close to God to bring him close to others, be sanctified to sanctify, lead by the hand and counsel prudently. I know whose ministers we are, where we find ourselves and to where we strive. I know God's greatness and man's weakness, but also his potential. [Who then is the priest?

He is] the defender of truth, who stands with angels, gives glory with archangels, causes sacrifices to rise to the altar on high, shares Christ's priesthood, refashions creation, restores it in God's image, recreates it for world on high and, even greater, is divinised and divinises.

> (St Gregory of Nazianzus, *Oratio*)
> (*CCC*: 1589)

St John Vianney, the famous parish priest of Ars, said this of the priest:

The priest continues the work of redemption on earth ... If we really understood the priests on earth, we would die not of fright but of love ... The Priesthood is the love of the heart of Jesus.

> (Jean-Marie Vianney, *Curé d'Ars*)
> (*CCC*: 1589)

A priest-friend of mine, we will call him Fr Jim, who spent most of his priestly life teaching in a school, was appointed by his bishop to a small rural parish in Ireland. Inexperienced in parish work, he decided after Mass one Sunday to consult the people as to what he should do in the parish. He approached a group of people, mostly farmers, and said to them, 'Men, what is it you want me to do here?' They looked at him, surprised to be asked such a strange question by their priest.

After a few moments of strained silence, one of them said, 'Well, Father, we really don't want you to do anything. We just want you to be here.'

I Will Come Myself

Fr Jim thought this was a wonderfully wise answer. It seemed that they, more than he, recognised Christ's presence in him and knew that there were things that only he could do for them. They wanted him to be there to baptise their children and to give them their First Communions. They wanted him to marry their sons and daughters, to bury the dead, and love them and pray for them, and in Confession lift the burden of their sins.

I have noticed where there is a community that no longer has a resident priest, the people seem very lonely. They feel bereft and vulnerable, literally 'like sheep without a shepherd'.

In my last years in Nigeria I had many beautiful experiences during my priestly ministry. I was sent to a parish of Atta where there had been no priests for several years. I arrived on the eve of the Feast of St Vincent de Paul to be greeted by a man who was the caretaker and cook. In the fading light I looked at the grass in the compound which was, to quote the words of the song, 'as high as an elephant's eye'. I ate my meal to the sound of a million cicadas and retired to bed in an empty mission house. In the morning I was awakened by hundreds of voices – men, women and children. I looked out the window and there they were. The grass was no more; the word had gotten around. *The Father is here*. There would be food. The children might live.

That very first day, a young man asked me to go to his village to minister to an old dying man named Joseph. I went on my little Honda motorcycle with this man sitting on the pillion. We travelled a few miles into the bush and arrived at the man's house. I will never forget this poor, venerable, dignified old man. He greeted me most warmly, 'Welcome, Father. I am happy that you have come. All my life I have prayed that I would not die without seeing a priest. I thank Jesus that He sent you to me, for today I am going to die.'

I talked to him for a little while. Then I heard his Confession and ministered to him the Anointing of the Sick, the Eucharist and the Apostolic Blessing, which carries with it a plenary indulgence at the moment of death. I then gave him his last Holy Communion in this world. When I had finished, he laid his head back on his pillow and said, 'Thank you, Father. Thank you, Jesus,' and died. It was very touching to witness the tender mercy of God towards this good man. The likelihood in those days of him having a priest at his deathbed was not great. Yet, here was I, not even twenty-four hours in the parish, the answer to his prayer.

When I came out of old Joseph's smoke-filled house, I was met by a group of over a hundred people. They looked like ghosts, like people from some Nazi death camp. Their clothing was ragged and filthy; most of them were covered with ugly, suppurating sores.

I asked Jude, my guide, 'Who are these people?'

He said, 'We are all lepers.'

'You, too?' I asked.

'Me, too.' He told me, 'The government sent us here and told us they would send food, medicine and clothing, but they never sent anything and we are suffering greatly.'

I was not surprised and uttered a quiet prayer to St Vincent de Paul that he would show me what to do.

Part of the work of priests and sisters at that time was to share out the meagre supplies of food and medicine that were being air-lifted into the country. There was never enough of anything, and here I was among these poor people who desperately needed me to do something for them. I returned to my mission house and loaded up my ancient Volkswagen Beetle with food and blankets, clothing and medicine, salt and soap, and whatever else I could find. And Jude the Leper and I returned to the village the next day.

The people were there to greet us, but they seemed passive and depressed. I thought they would be delighted and grateful to me for my effort on their behalf. In truth, I was annoyed by their lack of appreciation. When you are young, there are many things you do not understand. One of them is that when you serve the poor, they are a blessing to you and not the other way around. As I stood there I experienced another one of those moments when it seemed as if God spoke in my heart. With my hurt pride turning to anger against these poor people, I felt as if the Lord was saying to me, 'Yes, you have done what you can do. Now come and celebrate the Eucharist for them and let Me do what I alone can do.' And I knew on that hot, steamy afternoon that heaven had spoken and so I did what was asked of me. I arranged to come back two days later to celebrate Mass with Christ's suffering poor.

I was drowning in a sea of human suffering, but somehow these poor leprosy sufferers had a different quality to their misery. A few days later I went and celebrated Mass for them in the lean-to shelter that served as a church. I remember speaking to them on the Our Father and telling them of how God cares for and provides for His children. While I was delivering these exalted sentiments, my mind was in another place entirely.

I was thinking, why am I saying this to people who were experiencing nothing of this Divine beneficence? They were the poorest of the poor. They were ravaged with sickness. They were starving in a famine-stricken land, caught up in a vicious civil war that could overrun them any day. The atmosphere in the hut was sickeningly oppressive and I prayed I would survive until the end of Mass without getting ill.

Afterwards I went out into the afternoon sunlight and the fresh air. Usually, at the end of Mass people would come to greet the priest, but that day for some reason they stayed inside. I waited with the catechists for five, ten, fifteen minutes. I began to wonder if I had offended them and they were refusing to speak to me. I asked the catechist and he reassured me that I had not.

He said, 'How can they be offended when you spoke to them so beautifully about the love of the Father?'

Finally they began to emerge in ones and twos and did something very strange. Each of them came over to where I was standing and kissed my hands, an unusual gesture for Africans. Even the children performed this little ritual. I hardly knew how to react to this, but something told me that the reverence being offered was not for me but for Christ.

Finally, the head man of the village said, 'Father, on behalf of everyone in the village, I want to thank you that you brought Jesus among us once again.' At this, they all clapped and cheered and for the first time I saw smiles and joy and real happiness. The women were talking and laughing, the children playing and the men nodding in contented agreement.

As I stood there, the memory of the Lord's words came back to me, 'Come and celebrate the Eucharist for them and let Me do what I alone can do.'

It was a heart-melting moment. Jesus was present and had indeed done what only He could do. As I think back on it now, I see so clearly how our Lord Jesus had come among these desperately poor people and filled them with joy and peace, and the consolation of His Holy Spirit. He chose to do it through me, His priest. He willed that I make Him present through my ministry as a priest. They sensed this better than I did. They knew that Jesus had come to them in my words and above all, in the Holy Eucharist. They heard Him speak. They recognised Him 'in the breaking of bread' and their poor hearts burned within them.

My previous attempt to come to their aid was more about myself and my own ego than about helping the poor. But Jesus in His great mercy taught me a most valuable lesson. It was only when He showed Himself to me in them and let me see Him in my own priesthood that I was able to help them.

I will come Myself.

(Matthew 8:7)

We cannot help the poor without Christ. If we do not see Christ in the poor, we cannot help them. If we are not conscious of Christ within ourselves or if we are separated from Christ, we are just wasting our time. Jesus Christ will honour us when we serve Him in the poor. Jesus Christ is alive and He alone has the power to bring about peace and justice. Jesus Christ can do things that we cannot do. He can do through us what we ourselves are not able to accomplish. Movie stars and rock stars can generate a lot of publicity for various causes, but the road by which even they must travel to help the poor passes through the heart of Christ.

This connection to Christ comes to us by means of prayer. To go out to serve the poor, we must first humble ourselves before God in prayer.

Pope Benedict writes of this in his wonderful Encyclical *Deus Caritas Est*:

> Prayer, as a means of drawing ever new strength from Christ, is concretely and urgently needed. People who pray are not wasting their time, even though the situation appears desperate and seems to call for action alone. Piety does not undermine the struggle against the poverty of our neighbours, however extreme. In the example of Blessed Teresa of Calcutta we have a clear illustration of the fact that time devoted to God in prayer not only does not detract from effective and loving service to our neighbour but is in fact the inexhaustible source of that service. In her letter for Lent 1996, Blessed Teresa wrote to her lay co-workers: 'We need this deep connection with God in our daily life. How can we obtain it? By prayer.'
>
> It is time to reaffirm the importance of prayer in the face of the activism and the

I Will Come Myself

growing secularism of many Christians engaged in charitable work. Clearly, the Christian who prays does not claim to be able to change God's plans or correct what he has foreseen. Rather, he seeks an encounter with the Father of Jesus Christ, asking God to be present with the consolation of the Spirit to him and his work. A personal relationship with God and an abandonment to his will can prevent man from being demeaned and save him from falling prey to the teaching of fanaticism and terrorism. An authentically religious attitude prevents man from presuming to judge God, accusing him of allowing poverty and failing to have compassion for his creatures. When people claim to build a case against God in defence of man, on whom can they depend when human activity proves powerless?

(*Deus Caritas Est*: 36/37)

Before I took my leave of these poor stricken people, they came and said, 'Father, you must come again and bring the bishop with you next time. Many here have never been baptised or confirmed.'

I thank our Saviour that He allowed me to experience His presence at work through the sacraments of *my* priesthood and the Holy Eucharist. From that time I began to realise that all a priest has to do is let Jesus Christ work through him and provide Him every opportunity to do so.

Once, on a visit to Ars, I wrote this Prayer of a Priest:

> Lord Jesus,
> You abide in the Father
> and You abide in me.
> You anoint me with Your Spirit.
> You seal me
> with Your priesthood.
> You clothe me
> with Your image.
> Lord, speak through my voice,
> look through my eyes,
> listen through my ears,
> touch through my hands.
> At the breaking of bread
> may they recognise You not me
> may they hear You not me.
> Fill my out-stretched hands
> with Your life
> Your love
> Your mercy
> and Your healing. Amen.

Jesus does help His priests in every aspect of our priestly ministry. He does speak through us; He looks through us and touches through us. And as I have explained, He is the only one who can change the pain of the poor into joy in the Lord. He takes us into the presence of the Father. He fills us with the peace of the Holy Spirit. He gives us a desire for Himself in His sacraments; in His Body, the Church; in worship and prayer.

Chapter 8
In Remembrance of Me

O Sacred Banquet in which Christ is our
food; His passion is recalled; grace fills our
hearts; and we receive a pledge of glory to
come.

(St Thomas Aquinas)

The bogs and valleys of Ireland are dotted with ancient
Mass rocks. They mark the places where during times of
persecution people would gather and a priest, at great
peril to his own life, would come and celebrate the
Eucharist. These Mass rocks are part of the legend of
our Irish faith and the price people were willing to pay
to have the privilege of attending the Holy Eucharist.
It is very fitting that when the apparition took place at
Knock in 1879, the focal point of the apparition was
the altar and the Lamb, symbolising the Paschal
Mystery of the risen, victorious Christ surrounded by
adoring angels, and attended by Mary, the Queen of
Heaven; John, the Beloved Disciple; and the humble
presence of St Joseph.

For generations Irish Catholics have paid dearly to
sustain their priests and protect them from harm,
especially in times of persecution. The Irish people

knew long before the Second Vatican Council that the Eucharist was indeed the true centre of the whole Christian life (Cf. *Lumen Gentium* II; par. 12).

There is hardly anywhere now on the face of the earth, from Manchester to Mexico City, from Barcelona to Beijing, where people have not had to suffer persecution because of their faith in the Holy Sacrifice of the Mass, the Lord's Paschal Mystery.

Some years ago Sr Briege and I crossed into mainland China where it was arranged for us to meet people from the underground Church. We met a group of people, most of them young adults. Among them were two young priests who had travelled two days by train and bus to be with us. Through our guide and interpreter we spoke to them, celebrated Mass and prayed with them for a long time. During the Eucharist my mind was filled with the memory of Masses that were celebrated in other places, like the Mass rocks, like the secret Masses said in Britain by priests who were hunted down like animals and put to death. I thought of priests during the French Revolution and the Spanish Civil War, the priests on the run in Mexico and the hatred of the Eucharist that filled the hearts of their persecutors. The devotion of this little hidden congregation and of those two young concelebrating priests moved me and gave me an appreciation of the privilege I enjoy of being able to celebrate the Eucharist openly and freely.

I have a great friend from Eastern Europe who fled from her own country during the Second World War. She shared with me how she escaped from her village and that the last thing she saw there was her priest being nailed to the door of his church and riddled with bullets. She said, 'I will never forget the sight of his blood running down the steps of the church.' She went on to relate an incident which happened during a retreat that she attended in the United States. She told me that on the last day of the retreat, a young priest, dressed in blue jeans and a T-shirt, came out to celebrate Mass. She thought, charitably, surely at the Offertory he will put on his vestments. Not only did he not do that, but he proceeded to produce chocolate chip cookies and a bottle of Coca Cola instead of bread and wine. He raised the cookies and the coke bottle and began to pray the Offertory prayers.

'At this,' she said, 'I could contain myself no longer. I remembered my poor pastor nailed and bleeding. I got up, went over to the young priest and said, "Father, how dare you trivialise the Eucharist in this way. How dare you disrespect this sacrament for which so many priests and people have laid down their lives."'

People of strong faith in the Eucharist might not be able to give expression to it in words, but deep down they have a firm conviction of its meaning and importance. In the past many would walk for miles in the cold of winter to gather around a rock on an Irish hillside to hear the Word of God and receive the Body of Christ, their risen Saviour, in Holy Communion. Sadly, today many will not even drive their cars a few hundred yards to attend Sunday Mass.

Several years ago, a man came to me and said, 'Thirty years ago I came up to the city from the country to study law. At that time I and many of my classmates decided we had had enough of the Catholic Church, so I stopped going to Mass. Since that day I have never received Communion and never made my Confession and hardly ever prayed.'

I asked him, 'Why are you here then?'

'Some time ago,' he said, 'I was told I had an inoperable tumor of the brain. The doctor informed me that I had about three years to live. Recently the severe symptoms have returned and I am afraid my time may be getting short. You know, Father,' he said, 'when you are young, you think you know everything.'

'I know,' I said.

'And yet, strange as it may seem, I really have missed going to Mass because my parents were people of strong faith. It was just that I hadn't the courage to start again and I was afraid to risk the ridicule of my lapsed friends. The truth is I don't know what to do. I don't know how to come back to the Church because of all the changes that have taken place.'

I said, 'You know, the key that lets you back into the Church is Confession, and that has not changed.'

We talked for a while about how he might prepare for Confession. I gave him some things to read and some prayer leaflets and asked him to come back when he was ready. He returned a week later, and I heard his Confession and gave him his first Communion in thirty years. He was home again in the Church. After a few weeks his wife phoned to tell me that he had died. 'He asked me to let you know and thank you for the help you gave him,' she said.

We remember from our school English courses Francis Thompson's magnificent poem 'The Hound of Heaven' and those first chilling lines:

> I fled Him, down the nights and down the days;
> I fled Him, down the arches of the years;

I fled Him, down the labyrinthine ways
Of my own mind; and in the midst of tears
I hid from Him, and under running
laughter.
Up vistaed hopes I sped;
And shot, precipitated,
Adown Titanic glooms of chasmed fears,
From those strong Feet that followed,
followed after.
But with unhurrying chase,
And unperturbed pace,
Deliberate speed, majestic instancy,
They beat – and a Voice beat
More instant than the Feet –
'All things betray thee, whom betrayest
Me'.

For Francis Thompson, Jesus was the Hound of
Heaven. For all mankind, He is our merciful Saviour.
He is the Good Shepherd. He is the Bread of Life.

> I am the bread of life. Your fathers ate the
> manna in the wilderness, and they died.
> This is the bread which comes down from
> heaven, that a man may eat of it and not
> die. I am the living bread which came
> down from heaven; if any one eats of this
> bread, he will live for ever; and the bread
> which I shall give for the life of the world
> is My flesh.
>
> (John 6:48-51)

Some of the disciples could not grasp the reality of this
teaching of Jesus, as we read in John Chapter 6:

Many of His disciples, when they heard it, said, 'This is a hard saying; who can listen to it?' But Jesus, knowing in himself that his disciples murmured at it, said to them, 'Do you take offence at this? Then what if you were to see the Son of Man ascending where he was before? It is the spirit that gives life, the flesh is of no avail; the words that I have spoken to you are spirit and life. But there are some of you that do not believe.' For Jesus knew from the first who those were that did not believe, and who it was that should betray him. And he said, 'This is why I told you that no one can come to me unless it is granted him by the Father.' After this many of His disciples drew back and no longer went about with him. Jesus said to the twelve, 'Will you also go away?' Simon Peter answered him, 'Lord, to whom shall we go? You have the words of eternal life; and we have believed, and have come to know that you are the Holy One of God.'

(John 6:60-69)

The disciples, even though they believed in Jesus, must have wondered what He meant by this teaching. Their faith was confirmed at the Last Supper. We read in the Gospel of St Luke:

And when the hour came, he sat at table, and the apostles with him. And he said to them, 'I have earnestly desired to eat this passover with you before I suffer; for I tell you I shall not eat it until it is fulfilled in the kingdom of God.' And he took a cup, and when he had given thanks he said, 'Take this, and divide it among yourselves; for I tell you that from now on I shall not drink of the fruit of the vine until the kingdom of God comes.' And he took bread, and when he had given thanks he broke it and gave it to them, saying 'This is my body which is given for you. Do this in remembrance of me.' And likewise the cup after supper, saying 'This cup which is poured out for you is the new covenant in my blood.'

(Luke 22:14-20)

These words, 'This is My body which is given for you', 'This cup which is poured out for you is the new covenant in My blood' and 'Do this in remembrance of Me' have a depth of meaning that the disciples could only have grasped on later reflection because of the speed with which events began to unfold immediately after the Last Supper. Later, with the help of the Holy Spirit, they would know the meaning of the words 'of My blood poured out' when they saw it happen on Calvary. The disciples, being Jewish, would realise the unique meaning of covenant, a theme that runs through the history of the chosen people.

The Church from the very beginning has understood clearly what is encompassed in the celebration of the Lord's Supper. It is the Paschal

Mystery; that is to say, it is the celebration, the making present of the Lord's Supper. It is the sacrifice of the passion and death of Jesus on the Cross; it is also the celebration of the Christ's glorious resurrection from the dead. The Mass is all of these events made present sacramentally to the Church in every age. The Jesus who we receive sacramentally in Holy Communion is He who was scourged, who carried His Cross, who was crucified and rose from the dead on Easter Sunday morning. In the Sacred Liturgy the Church cries out, 'Behold the Lamb of God; behold Him who takes away the sin of the world. Blessed are those who are called to the supper of the Lamb.'

The Church obliges us to attend the Eucharistic celebration on Sundays and Holy Days. Unfortunately, many people no longer do this. Their faith has grown weak. And yet Jesus still invites us. He will never force us, but His heart is wounded by those who slight Him and turn away. 'Will you also go away?'

Peter answers for all of us, 'Lord, to whom shall we go? You have the words of eternal life; and we have believed, and have come to know that You are the Holy One of God' (John 6:68-69).

At Mass we hear the words of Jesus proclaimed. The Word of God proclaimed in the Eucharistic Liturgy is indeed the word of eternal life. It is the word that has the power to take sin from our hearts. It is the word that brings us healing and peace, and transforms us into the likeness of Christ. Pope Benedict XVI writes:

> The 'subject' of the liturgy's intrinsic beauty
> is Christ himself, risen and glorified in the

I Will Come Myself

Holy Spirit, who includes the Church in his work. Here we can recall an evocative phrase of St Augustine which strikingly describes this dynamic of faith proper to the Eucharist. The great Bishop of Hippo, speaking specifically of the Eucharistic mystery, stresses the fact that Christ assimilates us to himself: 'The bread you see on the altar, sanctified by the word of God, is the body of Christ. The chalice, or rather, what the chalice contains, sanctified by the word of God, is the blood of Christ. In these signs, Christ the Lord willed to entrust to us his body and the blood which he shed for the forgiveness of our sins. If you have received them properly, you yourselves are what you have received.' Consequently, 'not only have we become Christians, we have become Christ himself.' We can thus contemplate God's mysterious work, which brings about a profound unity between ourselves and the Lord Jesus: 'one should not believe that Christ is in the head but not in the body; rather he is complete in the head and in the body.'

(Sacramentum Caritatis: 36)

The disciples on the road to Emmaus recognised Jesus at the breaking of the bread as did the poor people of Penal Ireland and Elizabethan England. Even today in Communist China, Christians are experiencing Christ in their midst when the Sacred Host is raised. Unfortunately, many people today in the free world find it difficult to identify Christ in the Eucharist. In the age of the iPod and McDonald's, have we become deaf to God's word? Have we lost our appetite for the Bread of Life?

From the beginning, God has desired to draw near to us. He has longed to communicate something of His love for us 'poor, banished children of Eve'. Through Abraham and Moses, through the patriarchs and prophets, He has revealed His love for us. Finally, in His Son Jesus, God has revealed the fullness of His love. When Jesus wanted to illustrate the qualities of His Father's love, He told the *Parable of the Prodigal Son* (Cf. Luke 15:11-32). When Philip said to Jesus, 'Lord, show us the Father and we will be satisfied,' Jesus said to him, 'He who has seen Me, has seen the Father.' In other words, Jesus is saying, 'I am the perfect image and revelation of God My Father.'

Jesus gave His life for us in a most excruciating and horrific manner by dying on the Cross. He did this to undo the sins of mankind going back to Adam and Eve. He did it out of love for us, to show us how much His Heavenly Father was willing to do to save us. Jesus, in His body, took upon Himself the sins of the world. At the Last Supper He said, 'Do this in remembrance of Me.' At Mass Jesus makes Himself present to us at the Last Supper and at His passion, death and resurrection.

In the Eucharist we are united with our Saviour. Jesus takes our sins and sufferings up on the Cross and cleanses us in His precious blood. St Augustine, summing up the Church's teaching on the Eucharist, reminds us how completely we take part in the sacrifice of Jesus our Redeemer:

This wholly redeemed city, the assembly and society of the saints, is offered to God as a universal sacrifice by the high priest who in the form of a slave went so far as to offer himself for us in his Passion, to make us the Body of so great a head ... Such is the sacrifice of Christians: 'we who are many are one Body in Christ.' The Church continues to reproduce this sacrifice in the sacrament of the altar so well-known to believers wherein it is evident to them that in what she offers she herself is offered.

(St Augustine, *City of God*, 10, 6)

The Eucharist is the sacrifice of Christ and the sacrifice of the Church. The sacrifice of Christ on the Cross and the Eucharistic sacrifice of Christ on the altar are one single sacrifice. The Mass is not a repetition of the sacrifice of the Cross; it is one and the same. In the Eucharist, Christ's sacrifice becomes our sacrifice. Our lives, our praise, our prayer, our sufferings, our work are united with Christ and offered to the Father. So this Eucharistic sacrifice of Christ is present on every altar whether that altar is in a catacomb, a cathedral, an Irish bog or a Chinese apartment. And it is this same Eucharistic sacrifice that makes it possible for every generation of believing Christians to be united to Jesus Christ in His suffering and in His triumphant victory over sin and death.

Let me conclude with this quotation from Pope Benedict XVI:

> The Eucharist is the 'treasure' of the Church, the precious heritage that Her Lord has left to Her. And the Church preserves it with the greatest care, celebrating it daily in Holy Mass, adoring it in churches and chapels, administering it to the sick, and as *viaticum* to those who are on their last journey.
>
> However, this treasure which is destined for the baptised does not exhaust its radius of action in the context of the Church: the Eucharist is the Lord Jesus who gives Himself 'for the life of the world' (John 6:51). In every time and in every place, He wants to meet human beings and bring them the life of God. And that is not all. The Eucharist also has a cosmic property: the transformation of the bread and the wine into Christ's body and blood. It is in fact the principle of the divinisation of creation itself. For this reason the feast of Corpus Christi is characterised particularly by the tradition of carrying the most Blessed Sacrament in procession, an act full of meaning. By carrying the Eucharist through the streets and squares, we desire to immerse the bread come down from heaven in our daily lives. We want Jesus to walk where we walk, to live where we live; our existence must become his temple.
>
> (Pope Benedict XVI, Papal Address,
> 19 June 2006)

I Will Come Myself

Chapter 9
Say But the Word

> Lord do not trouble yourself, for I am not
> worthy to have you come under my roof;
> therefore I did not presume to come to
> you. But say the word, and let my servant
> be healed.
>
> (Luke 7:6-7)

Once on a visit to Brazil with Sr Briege, we were
conducting a healing service in a large indoor stadium
in Fortaleza. There were several thousand people
present. The Blessed Sacrament was exposed on the
altar for a period of singing, prayer and worship.
During a silent lull the pure voice of a little boy rang
out through the whole stadium. High up in the crowd
he cried out, 'Jesus, we love You! Jesus, we love You!'
It was like the prayer of an angel and everyone was
stunned by its beauty and the anointing of the Holy
Spirit that was upon this child.

Even more amazingly, when I began to carry the
Blessed Sacrament through that vast multitude of
people, this same little boy who had run down from
his place in the stands, walked backwards in front of

me looking up at the Sacred Host and saying, 'Jesus, we love You.'

When I began to work with Sr Briege we were faced with the problem of how best to conduct a healing service, which is such an integral part of Sr Briege's ministry. The first time the problem presented itself was when we were asked to pray with the Conference of Bishops in Korea. I said to Sr Briege, 'You and I cannot go around laying hands on bishops; it doesn't seem appropriate. Bishops are the ones who lay hands on people, not us.' It suddenly occurred to me that we should ask the bishops to come forward one by one and stand in front of the altar where the Blessed Sacrament was exposed, and we would stand one on each side of the bishop and pray silently for him. It was an inspiration of the Holy Spirit. It seemed a perfect way for Catholics to pray for healing. It focused on Jesus in the Blessed Sacrament – Jesus, who is the One who heals. In healing services for the laity, I would take the monstrance containing the Blessed Sacrament and move through the church, blessing the people as I walked slowly among them. During this Eucharistic procession, Sr Briege, from the podium, prayed for the healing of all present, inviting them to look at the Sacred Host and even stretch out their hands in prayer and pleading.

In Taiwan, a very old Chinese woman came out from the middle of the crowd and with slow arthritic movement knelt on the ground in front of the monstrance and kissed my feet. Everyone who saw her was moved to tears. I wondered who she was. Perhaps she had been deprived of the Eucharist for years. What kind of inner mystical life did she lead that allowed her

I Will Come Myself

to see the Eucharistic Christ so clearly and love Him so much? I will seek her out when I get to Heaven and have a talk with her.

Another time, a poor woman in the Philippines asked me what the words *'Et verbum caro factum est'* meant. She said, 'I know it is not English. What language is it?'

I said, 'It is Latin and it means "The Word was made flesh." Why do you ask?'

She replied, 'Father, when you are walking around with the Blessed Sacrament, those words appear in a semi-circle around you all the time.'

At a healing service in Kenya, there was a nine-year old boy, who when I blessed him with the monstrance, kept clapping his hands and speaking to Jesus in the Sacred Host. When I returned to the altar he came out of his pew and very reverently began to dance in front of the Blessed Sacrament. No one made any attempt to stop him. Eventually he stood there silently before the monstrance with his eyes closed and his hands joined. Afterwards some sisters told me that this boy had been paralysed with polio as a young child and that his father, that evening, had carried him several miles to bring him to the church. The poor know their need for God and when they turn to Him, He answers them.

Another time on an island in the South Pacific, there was a boy who had never spoken a word in the twelve years of his life. After the healing service he returned home and described in perfectly normal speech all that he had seen and heard.

The reality of the sacramental presence of Jesus in the Eucharist and in the Blessed Sacrament reserved in our tabernacles has been taught by the Church since the earliest times. It is a reality that people are coming to appreciate more and more in spite of the confusion caused by what some have written. Pope Benedict has set out to dispel this. He writes:

> One of the most moving moments of the Synod came when we gathered in Saint Peter's Basilica, together with a great number of the faithful, for eucharistic adoration. In this act of prayer, and not just in words, the assembly of Bishops wanted to point out the intrinsic relationship between eucharistic celebration and eucharistic adoration. A growing appreciation of this significant aspect of the Church's faith has been an important part of our experience in the years following the liturgical renewal desired by the Second Vatican Council. During the early phases of the reform, the inherent relationship between Mass and adoration of the Blessed Sacrament was not always perceived with sufficient clarity. For example, an objection that was widespread at the time argued that the eucharistic bread was given to us not to be looked at, but to be eaten. In the light of the Church's experience of prayer, however, this was seen to be a false dichotomy. As Saint Augustine put it: *'nemo autem illam carnem manducat, nisi prius adoraverit; peccemus non adorando –* no one eats that flesh without first adoring it; we should sin were we not to adore it.'

I Will Come Myself

In the Eucharist, the Son of God comes to meet us and desires to become one with us; eucharistic adoration is simply the natural consequence of the eucharistic celebration, which is itself the Church's supreme act of adoration. Receiving the Eucharist means adoring Him whom we receive. Only in this way do we become one with Him, and are given, as it were, a foretaste of the beauty of the heavenly liturgy. The act of adoration outside Mass prolongs and intensifies all that takes place during the liturgical celebration itself. Indeed, 'only in adoration can a profound and genuine reception mature. And it is precisely this personal encounter with the Lord that then strengthens the social mission contained in the Eucharist, which seeks to break down not only the walls that separate the Lord and ourselves, but also and especially the walls that separate us from one another'.

(*Sacramentum Caritatis*: 66)

This renewal of devotion to the Eucharist is the work of the Holy Spirit, drawing our attention to the True Presence of our Eucharistic Lord at a time when that Presence is being denied or ignored. Sr Briege and I receive many letters describing healings that have taken place during our Eucharistic healing services.

One woman wrote about the experience of her friend:

At the beginning of the praise, she began to weep and felt a strong sense of God's presence. During the Eucharistic procession she said that she felt a desperate need for relief, and when it looked as though Fr Scallon was not going to come her way, she called out 'Jesus, Jesus'. Fr Scallon then came over to her. She reached out and touched the monstrance and immediately began to rest in the Spirit. After resting in this way, she felt much better and experienced almost no pain at all. She put aside her cane and was thrilled that she felt so well. She knew she was different. She no longer had a desire to smoke. She had no more fear of discouragement. She said that she had learned a great lesson – that if you want God enough, you have to reach out to Him.

Another person wrote:

At that time I was taking a lot of painkillers. I had undergone extensive dental treatment because of a bone degeneration disease. The night of the healing service the pain was more severe than usual and even the painkillers had not been effective. As the monstrance with the Blessed Sacrament was being taken around the cathedral and stopped in front of the bench we were occupying, an intense joy and peace came over me. At that moment my pain vanished completely and to this day I have had no further problems, no pain and no need for treatment.

This is what a boy wrote:

> I write to tell you what happened at the retreat. I had a marvellous experience during the healing service. When the priest passed in front of me with the Eucharist, I had an extraordinary confidence that Jesus was in front of me, healing my heart, hearing my prayers, seeing me. I have always known that Jesus is in the Eucharist, but at that moment I could feel with total certainty. Since then I have changed my way of looking at the Eucharist.

Another woman wrote:

> My family has attended this conference every year for the last six years. The first year that we attended, Sr Briege McKenna and Fr Kevin Scallon were there. We were fallen-away Catholics with addictions of every kind and had only been in our conversion for about four months. At that time I was taking twenty-seven hundred milligrams of Lithium and fifty milligrams of Prozac a day for manic depression. During the healing service, when Fr Kevin was walking around with Jesus in the Most Blessed Sacrament, I thought if I could only 'touch the hem of his garment' I will

be healed as the woman with the haemorrhage (Cf. Luke 8:43-48). Well, I did touch the very end of his garment. After that, Sr Briege was calling out healings and as she said that Jesus was now healing someone with manic depression. I knew it was me. I actually felt the presence of Jesus flowing through me like 'Rivers of living water' (Cf. John 7:37-39). That night I threw away all my medication. My doctor told me that I could not do this without serious repercussions. He performed lithium level tests which came out normal and six months later they were still normal. I had been healed and have had no problem with mania or depression in six years!

A woman who was suffering from degenerative arthritis of the spine wrote:

At the Eucharistic Healing Service on Sunday morning, Fr Scallon processed with the monstrance through the convention center. With Steven on my lap, I began to cry uncontrollably. As Fr Scallon approached our row, I felt a warmth throughout my entire body and almost immediately the pain was gone. I was afraid to say anything even to my friend sitting beside me ... I felt that this miraculous healing could not be happening to me. But gradually I came to believe that this was a

I Will Come Myself

true confirmation of God's love for me. This has deepened both my faith and my prayer life.

Once at a conference in the United States, during a Eucharistic Healing Service, I was walking around blessing the people with the Blessed Sacrament. I stopped in front of a young woman with a baby; I blessed her and went on my way. The following day I received a phone call from this same woman asking me if I could see her for a few moments. When she arrived, she was overcome with emotion and proceeded to tell me what had happened the day before during the Eucharistic Healing Service.

She explained that when I stopped in front of her and blessed her with the monstrance, her little nine-month-old baby, Mary Kathryn, stood up, stretched out her hands toward the Blessed Sacrament and said, 'Hi, Jesus'. She did this twice, the first words she had ever spoken.

We should all pray to have the heart of a child, that we might be able to recognise our Eucharistic Lord. Mary Kathryn has grown up to be a beautiful faith-filled young woman and a powerful witness of her devotion to the Holy Eucharist.

Chapter 10
Jesus and the Red-headed Woman

I wondered how she had begun that day. Did she stand in the kitchen looking out the window, wondering, remembering her niece's little joke: 'Auntie Mary, our Sean says you swallowed a basketball'? After seven months of pregnancy it probably felt like that. Right then, it didn't seem so funny. Did she recall the dire warnings of her doctor to rest and stay at home? She remembered hearing about the healing Mass at Knock.

Did she debate, 'Will I or won't I? The doctor will kill me if he hears I went to Knock.'

Probably she prayed, 'Lord, you have taken care of me until now. Should I not trust You once more?'

Did a voice within her say, 'Go! Go in peace!'?

In any event, she went. At the church she thought, so far, so good, and slipped in at the back not far from the door, thinking, just in case, you never know. For me it was the last day of the Triduum, concluding with the Eucharist and prayers for healing. It is not possible to encounter Jesus Christ and not be healed on some level. I spoke that day about the healing presence of Christ in the Eucharist and prayed a long prayer for healing, enough to cover every infirmity of body, soul and spirit.

At Communion I stood at the front of the centre aisle and people came up to receive the Eucharist. After a few minutes I heard an inner voice say to me, 'Look at the woman with the red hair.' I was surprised by this but considered it might be just my overactive imagination, so I continued to distribute Holy Communion.

Again the inner voice said, 'Look at the woman with the red hair.' This time I did not ignore the instruction and looked down the line of people coming up for Communion. Halfway down the church there was a tall young woman with a magnificent head of red hair. When I looked at her, she looked up at me and then sat down in a pew. When eventually she came up to receive Holy Communion, I saw that she was pregnant.

In the sacristy after Mass I prayed, 'Lord, You better explain to me about this red-headed woman because I have a feeling she will be waiting for me in the church.'

The same inner voice said to me, 'Tell this young woman how much I love her and how much I appreciate all that she has suffered during this pregnancy.'

In obedience to the Lord's instruction, I went out into the church and sure enough, there she was, standing near the door. She came over to me and said, 'Father, can I speak to you for a moment, please?'

I said, 'Yes, but before you say anything to me, I have something to say to you. Jesus wants me to tell you how much He loves you and how grateful He is to you because of what you have suffered during this pregnancy.'

With that, her tears began to flow and she sat down. She said, 'Father, why did you look at me like that?'

'Like what?' I said.

'When you looked down the Church at me I felt this strange power pass through my entire body and into the child in my womb.'

'At that moment,' she said, 'I knew that everything was going to be all right. And when you put the Sacred Host on my tongue I felt completely enveloped in the love of God. I can't describe it but it was amazing and wonderful. As for the pregnancy, I can not begin to tell you how close and how often I have come to losing this child.'

I said to her, 'I do not know what the Lord has planned for you or your child, but I am sure that it must be something very special indeed.'

She left and I never saw her again.

Sometimes people wonder if the Lord is even aware of their presence when they come to Mass or to a healing service. Jesus sees everyone at every moment. He saw that young expectant mother all that day. He saw her in her kitchen and in her car. He saw her as she walked into the church. He saw her when she rose to go up for Holy Communion. He looked at her through the eyes of His priest and overwhelmed her with His loving presence in the Eucharist. He healed her, made safe her pregnancy and blessed the child in her womb.

I learned a lot that day. Once more Jesus let me see how present He is in my ministry as a priest. He *does* look through my eyes and He speaks with my voice and touches with my hands. Had I not risked responding to that inner voice, no doubt Jesus could have ministered to her in some other way, but He wanted to do so through His priest at the Holy Eucharist. I learned how necessary it is for me as a priest to have a listening heart and be led by the Holy Spirit in discerning the perfect will and plan of the Heavenly Father. *'I will come Myself'* (Matthew 8:7).

Chapter 11
You Did it to Me

The first time I *came under the surgeon's knife* was during my missionary days in Nigeria. I had returned home from a long parish mission and was awakened in the middle of the night with a severe pain in my side. I was rushed to a hospital run by the Medical Missionaries of Mary and a young English surgeon there removed my appendix. 'Just in time,' he told me later.

Years later in Ireland I had an operation on varicose veins. It involved long incisions on the back of both my legs just behind the knee. I do not recall how many stitches I had, but they were many. The next day, one of the religious sisters came in and told me I had to get up and go for a walk.

'We don't want you getting a clot now, do we?'

I protested, 'Sister, I can't even stand. How am I going to walk?'

'Oh, don't worry,' she said, 'you'll do fine.' I struggled out into the corridor with all the agility of Boris Karloff in the role of Frankenstein.

For the next few days, *Sister Bossy-boots* came in to get me ready for my 'walk' muttering something about 'your own good' and 'a lot worse off than you are' and other uplifting sentiments. But I was determined to be miserable; no one was going to crash my little pity party.

After a couple of days I returned to being a Christian and Sister was transformed from *Bossy-boots* to an *Angel of Mercy*. I asked her if I could celebrate Mass.

'You'll have to do it sitting down,' she said.

'That will be fine,' I replied.

She went on to tell me about Fr John.

She said, 'There is a priest in the room next to yours and he has not offered Mass for weeks. He was abroad in the missions and seems to have no one belonging to him. Maybe you could get him to concelebrate with you.'

I called on Fr John and asked him if he would like to concelebrate Mass with me. At first he seemed reluctant but in the end he agreed. I said, 'Between the two of us, Fr John, we'll be able to manage.' The next morning we went to the Oratory to prepare for Mass. The sisters had a system for counting the number of altar breads needed for Holy Communion at each Mass. They placed a box of hosts so that each person attending the Mass could place one into the ciborium to be consecrated.

All went well until we got to the Our Father. At that point, three visiting nuns came into the Oratory. I looked out at them and thought to myself, I hope these three nuns don't come up to Communion, because if they do I'm going to have to climb the steps to the tabernacle, take out a ciborium and come down again. I began to distribute Holy Communion and just when

I gave the last Sacred Host to the last person, the three nuns came up for Communion. My worst fears had been realised, and I resigned myself to the painful journey up to the tabernacle and down again. I turned around, and as I passed the altar I glanced again into the empty ciborium, and to my complete astonishment *it was no longer empty.* Now there were three hosts there, which I knew for certain were not there moments before!

My heart leaped within me because I knew that something miraculous had taken place right before my eyes. I turned and gave Communion to the three sisters.

In the sacristy after Mass, I stood on my stitched-up legs, stunned at what had just taken place. I began to pray, overwhelmed by a sense of gratitude, tears running down my face. I felt so blessed, so ecstatic, so grateful to my Eucharistic Lord, that I hardly knew what to do with myself.

I kept saying, 'Lord, why me? Why did You do this for me?'

A voice within me said, 'I did that for you because of what you did for Me in Fr John.'

Even writing about it all these years later, I still experience the deep emotion of this miraculous Eucharistic sign. 'And when did we see thee sick … and visit thee? And the King will answer them, "Truly I say to you, as you did it to one of the least of these my My brethren, you did it to me"' (Matthew 25:39-40). Christ is faithful to His promises. He was present to me in Fr John, He was present to Fr John in me and He was present to both of us in the Eucharist. How loving He was to this good priest in coming to him

My first Christian community

The saintly looking one on the right is me.

Second Mass, 29 May 1961

After my second Mass, 29 May 1961

Emmanuel's people, Nigeria, 1966

Retreat for priests in Malawi, late 1970s

With Sr Briege McKenna in Kenya, 1997

Retreat for priests in Ghana, 1989

Retreat for priests in Malaysia, 1993

Retreat for priests in Kenya, 1995

Retreat for priests in Japan, 1998

Eucharistic Healing Service

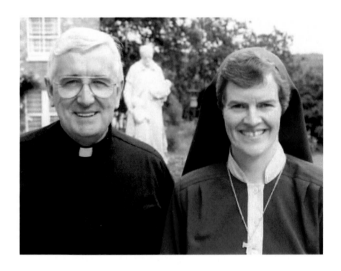

With Sr Briege McKenna in London, June 1998

With His Holiness Pope John Paul II in September 2000

Retreat for priests in Indonesia, 2005

'There's more to life ...' Visit with Mother Abbess M. Theresa, O.Cist., and the Sisters of the Cistercian Heart of Mary Abbey in Sostrup, Denmark

Eucharistic Procession through the streets of Ars
International Retreat for Priests, September–October 2005

through my invitation to once again concelebrate the Eucharist. How unbelievably loving He was to me with my stiff painful gait, to serve me by multiplying His Eucharistic presence. This is how real Jesus Christ is to us. These are the ways in which He delights in loving us. He loves each of us in a personal and individual way.

> So they drew near to the village to which they were going. He appeared to be going further, but they constrained him, saying, 'Stay with us, for it is toward evening and the day is now far spent.' So he went in to stay with them. When he was at table with them, he took the bread and blessed, and broke it, and gave it to them. And their eyes were opened and they recognised him; and he vanished out of their sight. They said to each other, 'Did not our hearts burn within us while he talked to us on the road, while he opened to us the scriptures?'
>
> And they rose that same hour and returned to Jerusalem; and they found the eleven gathered together and those who were with them, who said, 'The Lord has risen indeed, and has appeared to Simon!' Then they told what had happened on the road, and how he was known to them in the breaking of the bread.
>
> (Luke 24: 28-35)

Chapter 12
Letters from 'My Daughter'

It was Holy Week and I had offered to help the local priest with Confessions. The school retreat was finished, so I had time before leaving the next day. She was the first into the confessional, a student about twenty years old. Having finished her Confession, she began to tell me about herself. Mindful of the people waiting, I offered to meet her the next day when I would have more time to listen to her. She came to the priests' house and I heard her tale of great suffering. Before she left, when I was saying good-bye to her, she grasped my hand in her two hands and just stood there in silence with tears running down her fresh young face.

'Can I keep in touch with you?'

'Of course you can,' I replied. And she wrote down my address and telephone number. This was before the era of cell phones and email.

That was the one and only time I ever saw this girl. At the time, she was going to college. Her suffering was three-fold. First, there was the terrible pain of the tragic loss of both of her parents in an accident. Then there was the suffering caused by a traumatic childhood experience. In addition to all of that, she suffered severe physical pain related to a heart condition.

Soon after, there began a steady flow of letters and phone calls. She gave her address as 'my room' with the day and date. When she phoned, it was always from a public telephone. It seemed she wanted me to know nothing about her, not even her name. She signed herself as Mary, but I'm not sure if that was her real name. Her letters were long and newsy, about the things that she was doing in college. A lot of what she wrote was about her frequent visits to the hospital and her enforced periods of bed rest. She had her own car and often escaped from the home of her foster parents who, it seemed, had little interest in her. All of this caused her great emotional, spiritual and physical suffering.

Not having her address, I was not able to answer any of her letters. This was all right with Mary. She was happy enough to talk on the phone. After a few weeks I realised that she was talking to me the way that any young girl might talk to her dad. I knew that her first meeting with me had helped her a great deal, but she still struggled with her faith. Like so many sinned-against people, Mary was inclined to blame everything on herself.

Once she wrote, 'I don't know what to believe in. The fears and the hurt in my life are there in a greater or lesser way. It is only when I am able to stop, as I am doing now writing to you, knowing that you care enough to read this ... It is now that I feel safe. This means far more to me than anything the doctors are able to do. Who I am, or anything else does not matter to me ... what I fear is that it may matter to you, but that is something else. Just now I want us to be friends. I would like to think that you are behind me, but I guess I am on my own for this time.'

She kept promising to come to see me.

She finished this letter by saying, 'I have decided that I cannot come to visit you until I have put on a few pounds and have lost this desperate color that everyone tells me that I have. I am fairly wrecked just now, but with a little time and rest I'll soon be back to normal. You'll hear from me again soon. Hope you're not working too hard. This heat is awful.' She always signed off with 'In trust, Mary'.

Mary was a very bright girl who loved college and topped her class most of the time. Her poor health and frequent illness caused her great frustration.

She wrote to me after one of her phone calls: 'Good to talk to you this morning. I'm sorry I had to go. I am doing very badly with the books. It is hard to concentrate and this dead heat only adds to things. Father Kevin, I am so glad I have you now. I haven't felt alone very much. I always think you are looking after me even though you are miles away. I am glad you don't know my name ... maybe now you will believe me when I tell you that it is not important. You may not hear from me for a while, but don't worry, I'll be thinking of you. And if things get too much for me, I can ring you. Thanks for everything ... In trust, Mary.'

On another occasion she wrote, 'I wasn't going to tell you, but I am too honest. I wanted to see you, but couldn't commit myself. So after talking to you on the phone, I decided I had to see you. I drove out to where you were giving a parish mission on Friday. Just seeing you was enough. I would like to have talked with you, but you were busy and I felt safe enough. The chance of you seeing me was limited; besides you might not have known me.'

After her first year in college, Mary became too ill to continue even though she desperately wanted to. Her heart got worse and she was in constant pain in spite of taking many painkillers. She continued to write me lengthy letters about her illness and her family life and her frequent visits to the hospital.

My communication with Mary, such as it was, taught me many things. The most important thing I learned was that we priests have little knowledge or insight into the impression we make on people or the kind of impact we have on their lives. As I look back on my own life, I can see what a huge impact priests and the ministry of priests had upon me from my first Confession, Mass, my education, right through to my Ordination and beyond. All the important events in my life were somehow connected to priests. I know now that what I was experiencing was the presence of Jesus Christ in every priest. People look to the priest because somehow they know that through him they will find Christ. No matter how despondent I may feel as a priest because of my sinful humanity, I must never forget that Christ is never limited by my sins or shortcomings.

Without my knowing it or even becoming aware of it, God the Father showed Himself through me, His priest, to this suffering girl and allowed her to experience the security of His Fatherly love. This is what Mary wrote to me in May of 1982: 'I hear you are in the hospital just now. I have two wishes for you: one, that you may have no pain; and two, that you may recover quickly. For these I pray, if my prayers are any good. I will worry about you until I hear you on the phone again, so I hope it won't be long. I never thought I would meet anyone who would mean even half as much as you do now. And it is not just because you are sick that I am writing this. In a way, I wanted to let go and say, "Father Kevin, you're a real friend." But you've got to see that this is a new experience for me. So you've got to be a little more patient with me until I get used to it. I don't understand it much – I met you twice, I've written to you and talked to you on the phone, and yet I trust you more than anyone else in the world. You know me better than anyone else.'

The letters and phone calls kept coming as Mary grew weaker and weaker. She wrote this to me from the hospital: 'Fr Kevin, I have been trying to figure out what to say to you about my health. I want to be fair to you, so after considerable thought I have decided that the truth is the only way to be fair. So, the story is not good. The operation failed to do its job. Another operation is too risky. They have done all they can for me. With a lot of rest and looking after, the doctor told me I could live for a year or more, but he wouldn't commit himself. He said that it was out of his hands. Each day could be my last. So you see, you are backing a very poor runner. The odds are against me.'

On another occasion she wrote, 'I am trying to decide what to do about you. You have become so important to me, it scares me. I am not sure I can keep hiding from you, but I have to. I need you more than you will ever know, but I am afraid. I do love you in my own crazy way. I trust you, but not myself. But I know you will help me.'

Once she asked me to pray for her friend Maria.

She wrote, 'Maria knows that I have a friend called Kevin. Once when I was ill in the hospital I was asking for you, in my delirium. Maria came to see me and the nurse asked her if she knew anything about Kevin. Maria said nothing to me about this until much later. So I said, "I have a friend called Kevin." But I said no more than that.'

During my life as a priest I have marvelled at how the Lord has worked so seamlessly through my priestly ministry. These months of contact with Mary were like that. I had met this nineteen-year old girl just once and yet the Lord had forged an amazing bond between us. To this day I am in awe of how the Heavenly Father took her into His loving embrace. She had lost both of her parents at a very young age and she had suffered greatly because of this. No one had been able to fill this empty space in her life until the Lord Himself decided to act. Little by little she began to unfold like a flower. She often told me that she did not know what love was. She had never experienced love and did not know how to love. It is only God who can heal this kind of wound and it is only Jesus who can fill this void. Christ is in every baptised person with the Father and the Holy Spirit. Through Baptism, they become members of His Body. But Christ is in the ministry of His priests in a way that goes beyond His presence in all the baptised. Through his ordination, a man is uniquely configured to Jesus Christ, the head of the body. Henceforth he represents Jesus Christ, the head of the body, whether he is aware of it or not.

Looking back, I realise that in this correspondence with Mary, in all those phone calls and letters, God was dealing with me too. He was teaching me how to be a father. I learned not to be afraid, to own the divine fatherhood in which as a priest I had been called to participate.

I have often told priests, especially young priests, 'Don't be afraid to be a father. People young and old want you to be a father to them. They don't want you to be a drinking buddy or some kind of back-slapping ordained teenager.'

The priest is a father because he is united to Jesus Christ, the Son of the Eternal Father. Jesus said, 'I am in the Father and the Father is in Me' (John 14:11). So it is with me the priest; the Father is in me and I in the Father. Now more than ever, people need to see and experience the love of the Heavenly Father in the priest. They need to experience God's fatherly love and mercy. Through the awful things that have happened, the enemy of Christ has tried to destroy the living image of God's fatherhood in priests. Priests should know the Father and honour Him. People should always be able to see the Father's kindness and gentleness through the ministry of priests.

In one of our phone conversations, Mary was lamenting about being left alone so much. 'No one cares about me. Nobody loves me. How could they?'

I said to her, 'But Mary, I love you. You know that.'

There was a silence on the other end of the phone and then she said with a tremble in her voice, 'Look, I'll phone you soon again.' And she hung up.

Her next letter ended not with her usual 'In trust, Mary', but with 'Much love, Mary.' Did I love her? Of course I did. How could I not? Did she know that I loved her? Thank God she did.

If I asked what I have missed most because of my vow of celibacy, my answer would be 'a daughter'. There is something about the relationship between father and daughter that is immensely appealing. So I would love to have had my own daughter. That, alas, is part of the sacrifice I knew I would have to make when I took my vow of celibacy. True to His promise, the Lord has given me many daughters and sons in every part of the world and they have never failed to enrich my life.

In her last letter to me, Mary poured out her heart. She wrote, 'Friendship needs no words. It is solitude delivered from the anguish of loneliness. I think that is a good definition of our friendship. I have come such a long, long way since knowing you. Why did I not meet you sooner? Why do I trust you more than anyone else? Why must I die without seeing you again? I know you will say that it is my decision, but you must understand that for you to see me now would mean that you would see only a shadow of a person you once met, early one Easter morning.

'Do you remember the day I rang you from the airport? I had just come back from the Canary Islands. I wanted so much to meet you then. But I was so weak I could barely stand. Remember the day I rang you in Dublin, you begged me to go to see you, but I wouldn't? I wanted to, but I was afraid I'd embarrass you because I was beginning then to have difficulty moving and coordinating. When I saw you that evening I was really happy; you didn't have to know I was there. Another time I rang you from hospital, only I didn't tell you where I was.

'Father Kevin, I don't want to die now that I know somebody really cares about me. God has helped me keep going and He sent you ... I've permitted myself one box, to put things in for you. These things are of great value to me. That's why I want you to have them. The Monchichi doll, his name is Paul; he's been with me for five years. I used to suck my thumb and hold Paul when the pain was bad. He's been a good friend. The tape is just the sort of music I like; I've spent many, many nights listening to tapes. *Mon Ami* is as the name suggests. The ash tray is just a token from my holiday which you were part of. The book is to represent all the books which I have read; the tennis-ball all the games I've played and enjoyed so much. I wanted to give you my camera, but its parts won't fit. So the postcards are to show you that I have seen great beauty and am grateful. The box is to represent the letters I've written to you. You'll wonder at the box because nearly all the letters you've received from me have been written on pages from my notebook or folder. The box itself [a candy box] is important because it, in a small way, represents the work I did for a short while. I enjoyed the business side of work and I loved meeting the small children who came in for sweets on their way to school. I'll put this pen in too, as it has been a great friend to me, enabling me to keep in touch with you. My writing to you has been so important. The box is not full because I can never, never let you know how much I have come to love and trust you. The space is there to be filled by those who will love you and trust you when I am gone.

'Father Kevin, the hurt is all gone now. I realise that all my life I have been the victim of circumstance. If my parents hadn't died, everything would've been so different. Now I must finish. Now that you will be away for five weeks, I want you to know that, no matter what happens, I do love you. It is hard for me to write that, as you know by now. I will ring you on February 5th at twelve noon, if God spares me until then. If not, someone will ring. I am not sure yet who I may delegate. Whatever happens, remember that by chance we met and by chance we can not meet again. I love you and trust you and will never forget your kindness. For some reason I haven't told anyone about you. You are very much a secret. I think I would like to keep it that way; our friendship will be very special then. Must go now. Very tired, very tired.'

Knowing that I would be away for five weeks and suspecting that she might die before my return, she did what she had never done before; she sent me an address at which I could write to her. I wrote her a letter. When she received my letter, she would not allow it to be opened. She held it in her hand for a couple of days. Eventually she asked her friend Maria to open it and read it to her. She listened to it, again and again, almost continuously until the end.

On 5 February I had a phone call from Mary's cousin to tell me that Mary had died peacefully in her sleep.

Chapter 13
I Am the Resurrection and the Life

When Martha heard that Jesus was coming, she went and met him, while Mary sat in the house. Martha said to Jesus, 'Lord, if you had been here, my brother would not have died. And even now I know that whatever you ask from God, God will give you.' Jesus said to her, 'Your brother will rise again.' Martha said to him, 'I know that he will rise again in the resurrection at the last day.' Jesus said to her, 'I am the resurrection and the life; he who believes in me, though he die, yet shall he live, and whoever lives and believes in me shall never die. Do you believe this?' She said to him, 'Yes, Lord; I believe that you are the Christ, the Son of God, he who is coming into the world.'

(John 11:20-27)

I rushed from our community dinner table. A man was dying in the hospital where I was chaplain. I had been attending him for some weeks trying to fan into flame the dying embers of his faith. Poor old Bill was well past eighty. He told me that when he was a young man he served in the British Army and was stationed in Ireland during the Easter Rising and the Civil War. 'Queer lot, them Irish,' he used to say. He did not seem to connect Irish-ness with me in spite of my accent. Here he was now, making his last Confession.

At the far end of the ward, one of the other patients was listening to his radio. A familiar voice and a familiar song mingled with the ritual Latin prayers:

> *Intróeat, Dómine Jesu Christe, domum hanc*

> Bright lights city, gonna set my soul, gonna set my soul on fire

> *qui custódiat, fóveat, prótegat, vísitet, atque deféndat*

> And they're all livin' devil may care

> *Per istam sanctam Unctió + nam*

> A fortune won and lost on every deal and all you need's a strong heart and a nerve of steel

> *Indúlgeat tibi Dóminus quidquid per gustum et locutiónem deliquísti*

> Viva las Vegas, viva las Vegas

> *Indulgentiam Plenarium*

> Viva, viva las Vegas

No one ever told me in the seminary that it might be like this. No family members gathered around, no murmured prayers. Just Elvis and 'Viva Las Vegas'.

I stumbled through the rituals of the last sacraments believing that in this contest between the 'king' and the King of Kings, Jesus, not Elvis, would prevail. Jesus had come for old Bill, who seemed happy enough to go.

Death is the final chapter for all of us. Some know when sister death will come. They see her down the long corridor of a prolonged final illness. Others meet her suddenly. One moment they are not feeling well; the next they are standing before their Heavenly Redeemer. The old preachers often use the text, 'In all you do, remember the end of your life, and then you will never sin' (Sirach 7:36).

As a boy growing up in Ireland I frequently attended funerals. That was before undertakers became funeral directors and coffins became caskets. There was no artificial carpet around the grave and no purple cushions to cover the coffin. To my dying day I will never forget the clatter of stony clay on the lid of a coffin as sturdy local men filled in the grave. It was a sound that had a powerful finality about it and one that caused many a strong man to mend his ways.

People today seldom cast their mind forward to the moment of their death. They forget that they will some day, maybe sooner than they realise, stand in judgement before God. If they did, their lives might be very different. It is so much better to meet Jesus as a lifelong friend than as a complete stranger. People who have lived at a distance from God may not find it easy to draw near to Him at the hour of death. Often times such a person will belong to a family which is equally distant from God, and which has no religious sense, and knows little of the ordinary pious customs and prayers that are so important at this time. They do not know what to do at that critical moment of the death of their loved one and consequently they experience little of the consolation that religion and prayer provide.

This is not to say that the dying person will not be saved and go eventually to heaven. If he is reconciled with the Lord, he will be saved, but will probably have to undergo the purification of Purgatory. I imagine Purgatory to be like a great rehabilitation hospital. When people have been in an accident or have had a stroke, they undergo physical therapy. People are happy to endure this, even though it involves considerable pain, so that they may return to normal health and mobility. A significant aspect of the suffering of Purgatory consists in the pain of remorse and regret over the sins and wrongdoing of a lifetime. The experience of Purgatory is not one of God's punishment, however, but of His mercy. Souls there know that they are destined for eternal life.

One mystic has written that there are different levels in Purgatory – the deepest a place of intense suffering and the highest at the threshold to Heaven. The existence of Purgatory cannot be denied, since, like the Church's teaching on Hell, it too is a defined dogma of our faith. Anyone who denies the existence of Purgatory or Hell is no longer in full communion with the faith of the Catholic Church.

There is hardly a day that I do not think about death. This is not a morbid preoccupation on my part.

The truth is that I look forward to my death, since it is the doorway that leads to eternal life. The path to that doorway – well, that is another matter. Will it be a short path or a long one? Maybe it will be just a step. Who knows?

Very many people fear death and will do anything to distract themselves from thinking about it. Suffering, too, frightens them. Years ago I visited two people in a hospital in the United States. One was a Polish-American woman, a mother of seven children who just had her cancerous larynx removed. She was receiving radium treatment and was in a lot of pain. I talked to her about redemptive suffering, about how through prayer and especially through the Holy Eucharist she could offer even the smallest pain to Christ on the Cross and that He could change this into redemptive grace and bring about the salvation of many souls. I explained that she could choose to experience her pain either as redemptive suffering or just plain human misery. She was obviously a woman of faith who had little difficulty believing me. I could see that this faith had already helped her to enter into the Paschal Mystery of Christ.

Down the corridor from her was a very wealthy man who was dying of lung cancer. He was filled with bitterness for everyone. He hated his wife and he especially hated his children. 'All they want is for me to die so they can get their hands on my money.' He was probably right. He told me that he had not been to a church for over forty years.

I said to him, 'You know, you should go to Confession to me right now.'

'I wouldn't know where to begin,' he growled.

'Don't worry. I'll help you,' I replied.

To my amazement he said, 'Would you?'

'Gladly,' I said.

The palpable presence of our Lord Jesus Christ filled that room with His mercy, forgiveness and healing for this sick, embittered man. His tears were very real and the peace that came upon him was the kind that only Christ can impart.

'*I will come Myself* [and cure him]' (Matthew 8:7). This man had known little peace in his miserable, affluent life. Now he had a peace that no one, not even his family, could take from him.

The dying of a loved one should be like a retreat for the family. It ought to be a time of repentance for the whole family and not just for the person dying. Old family sins should be forgiven and wounds healed, and silence and coldness ended by the presence of the merciful Christ. Where possible, a dying person should be surrounded and enveloped in an atmosphere of peace and prayer, as well as loving care. All family members should be willing to play their part so that the memory of those days and hours will be a comfort to them later on.

Recently I came across the homily that I preached at the funeral Mass of my eighteen-year old nephew who was killed tragically in a motor accident. I include it here in the hope that it may bring a moment of comfort to all who mourn the death of a child:

> There is an incident in St Luke's Gospel when Jesus was entering the town of Nain and He meets, coming out of the town, the funeral procession of a young man, the

only son of his widowed mother. Jesus' attention was drawn to the woman. He was filled with compassion for her. He did not attempt to explain what was happening to her. He did not say, 'Let me tell you what is happening here and why your son is dead.' No. The Gospel tells us simply that His heart went out to her.

People often ask: 'Why does God allow such things to happen?' To that question I have no answer. Yes, I could say to a mother, 'God took your son to Himself.' And if she were to say, 'I would rather He had left him here with me,' could I disagree with her? Could anyone? My own tears tell me, as yours tell you, that there are no words to explain these things.

But God does not cause accidents. I know that the God who is revealed to us in Jesus Christ is a God who weeps when a young son dies, that He is a God who has compassion for mothers who cry and for fathers who cannot hold back their tears, that He is a God who is filled with love for sisters and brothers whose hearts are broken with grief, and that He comforts poor priests who can find no words to explain.

Almost eighteen years have passed since we brought Oliver here to be born again in the waters of Baptism. I never wanted to see this day. I would rather that he would be the one to weep for me.

In the Gospel which we have heard, Martha speaks to Jesus about her brother who has just died. 'Lord, if You had been here my brother would not have died.' Jesus, who was so moved at the death of Lazarus, His friend, that 'He wept,' says to Martha, 'Your brother will rise again. I am the Resurrection and the Life. Anyone who believes in me, even though he dies, will live, and will never die. Do you believe this?' (John 11:21-26). No explanation, no trying to make sense of things; simply an invitation to childlike faith in the face of mystery. And Martha replies for all of us who believe. 'Yes, Lord,' she said, 'I believe that You are the Christ, the Son of God, the One who is to come into the world.'

Jesus' proclamation 'I am the Resurrection and the Life' is not mere empty words, but a pledge and a promise that gives hope to every human heart in the face of death. To Martha and Mary, Jesus gives them back their brother. To the grief-stricken widow of Nain, He returns her son, so that all people in every age would know that a day will come when every parent will find again their lost child. Every family will come to know the peace and the healing grace of Christ in a loving reunion that will never end.

In a world that tries so hard to deny death, we nevertheless live daily with its sadness. We do not deny death because we hope in the Lord who has said that 'Whoever lives and believes in Me will never die.' Even in life, families get separated by distance and time. But in the end, at death, we all come home to be with Jesus and Mary who gather us around the Table of the Bread of Life.

Oliver, we hardly knew you. Your life, like a falling star, come and gone in a blaze of light. But many there are who knew you – your own peers who are here to mourn with us today. They knew you and loved you well. They knew you as one they could rely on, as a loyal friend. You were the one to get things done; you took people as you found them; you could forgive sincerely. You understood how to comfort, how to bring healing. You brought people together, most notably on this sad day when we gather to mourn your going from us.

We will miss your smile and your gentle wit. This December day is darker without you. We will never forget you, little brother, and the light you brought to us all. Your beauty, now that you are with Christ, surpasses anything we ever saw in you. And strange as it may seem, your passing has made you more present to us than ever. May God receive your gentle soul and may He comfort your father and your mother, your brothers and your sisters, and all of us who loved you well.

I Will Come Myself

I concluded the homily with this ancient Irish prayer
for the dead:

> O Lord, may you free him from sin and
> lead him to heaven.
> Ease his sufferings,
> Increase his glory.
> Bestow upon his soul a drop of the dew of
> heaven
> And a drink from the spring of grace.
> So too on our souls at the hour of death.
> May his sufferings be lessened,
> His glory increased,
> May the light of glory shine on him
> And may he live in peace.
> Jesus, Heart of compassion,
> Grant to him and to us also everlasting
> happiness.
> May the Three oldest and youngest,
> The Three of highest rank in the city of
> glory
> Come to show us the way to heaven
> And take our souls there with him.
> I put you yesterday under Mary's
> protection.
> Today I put you under the protection of
> her only Son.
> May Peter freely open to you the gates of
> paradise.
> May Michael not call you to the left-hand
> side.
> May God and Mary come to seek you
> And may they bring your soul with them
> to the city of the saints.

O Virgin pure and fair
Whose Son was condemned in his Passion,
Beseech the King of graces
To grant forgiveness to us and to all
And to everyone who needs it.

I Will Come Myself

Chapter 14
Jesus the Divine Physician

> Truly, truly, I say to you, he who believes in
> Me will also do the works that I do; and
> greater works than these will he do,
> because I go to the Father. Whatever you
> ask in My name, I will do it, that the Father
> may be glorified in the Son; if you ask
> anything in My name, I will do it.
>
> (John 14:12-14)

An Irish writer, lapsed from his Catholic faith, was asked in a radio interview if there was anything that he missed from his life as a practising Catholic. He immediately replied, 'I miss Confession.'

When asked why, he said, 'Well, I never experience having my guilt taken away and my sins forgiven the way I used to when I went to Confession.'

He was right, of course. No therapy or counselling can bring about this kind of grace-filled experience. This happens in the Sacrament of Penance where we encounter the living, risen Christ, the same Jesus who said to the paralytic, 'Your sins are forgiven you.'

Jesus, after He rose from the dead, appeared to the disciples in the upper room. It is described for us in John's Gospel:

> On the evening of that day, the first day of the week, the doors being shut where the disciples were, for fear of the Jews, Jesus came and stood among them and said to them, 'Peace be with you.' When he had said this, he showed them his hands and his side. Then the disciples were glad when they saw the Lord. Jesus said to them again, 'Peace be with you. As the Father has sent me, even so I send you.' And when he had said this, he breathed on them, and said to them, 'Receive the Holy Spirit. If you forgive the sins of any, they are forgiven; if you retain the sins of any, they are retained.'
>
> (John 20:19-23)

It was as if He said to them, 'I am giving you the first fruits of My Passion, Death and Resurrection; namely the power to forgive sins.' Jesus wanted this power to be exercised in the Church for all time, knowing how much we would need a means by which we could come to Him and be forgiven. That access to the forgiving Christ is ours in the Sacrament of Reconciliation. This sacrament is a meeting with Jesus Christ, who through the ministry of the priest reconciles us to the Father and with one another.

I thank Jesus for all the times in my life that I have been able to kneel before a brother priest in

Confession, knowing in faith that I was coming to Jesus Christ Himself, whose mercy and forgiveness I was sure to receive.

People often say to me, 'I don't need to confess my sins to a priest. I can confess directly to God.'

We can confess directly to God, but since we belong to the Church, it is the will of Christ that we be reconciled to the Father through Him in this Sacrament of Reconciliation. The truth is that there is something very natural and human about Confession. Bartenders hear great confessions, as do hairdressers. Therapists and counsellors have discovered what the Church has known for centuries – that it is good to talk about your troubles. It is a human thing to do.

Some time ago I was waiting in a queue at a bank in the US when a young man came and stood behind me. He said, 'Hi' and I said, 'Hi'. He then proceeded to tell me that he was just out of 'rehab' and went on to make one of the best Confessions I have heard in years. When he finished, I felt like saying, 'Kneel down there and I will give you absolution,' but of course that wasn't possible, even though it was exactly what he needed. He desperately needed to be forgiven for the pain and hurt he had inflicted on himself and others. I am sure that there was some providence in the fact that he shared his troubles with me and not someone else. I have often prayed for him.

The Sacrament of Reconciliation really is the best of therapies. In my years as a priest I have observed that in the past when people went to Confession once a month, they were much healthier morally, emotionally and spiritually than they are now. The words of the prayer of absolution that the priest prays cast light on the Church's understanding of this sacrament:

> God, the Father of Mercies,
> through the death and resurrection of His Son
> has reconciled the world to Himself
> and sent the Holy Spirit among us
> for the forgiveness of sins;
> through the ministry of the Church
> may God give you pardon and peace,
> and I absolve you from your sins
> in the name of the Father, and of the Son,
> and of the Holy Spirit.
>
> (Rite of Penance)

We pray to God, the Father of Mercies, who has reconciled the world to Himself. He has done this 'through the death and resurrection of His Son'. This forgiveness of our sins is brought about by the sending of the Holy Spirit. This divine forgiveness is mediated to us by the ministry of the Church in the person of the priest who, taking the place of Jesus says, 'I absolve you from your sins in the name of the Father, and of the Son, and of the Holy Spirit.'

The priest may then say the final prayer of the Sacramental Rite:

> May the Passion of our Lord Jesus Christ,
> the intercession of the Blessed Virgin Mary,
> and all the saints, whatever good you do
> and suffering you endure heal your sins,
> help you to grow in holiness, and reward
> you with eternal life.

This prayer, 'Heal your sins,' echoes the incident in the Gospel where the paralytic was let down through the roof and Jesus said to him, 'Your sins are forgiven.' This maddened the scribes, who said, 'Only God can forgive sins.' But Jesus, to prove that He had the power to forgive sins, said to the man, 'Rise, take up your pallet, and go home' (Mark 2:11). And he did.

For many, the Sacrament of Reconciliation is a real encounter with Christ, as I know from all the time I have spent hearing Confessions. I have seen people's lives profoundly healed in ways that only Christ could do.

That Gospel story of the paralytic reminds me of something that happened during a week-long parish retreat that Sr Briege and I conducted in a town in the United States. As with all our retreats, the first day is dedicated to the Sacrament of Reconciliation.

On the Friday morning of the retreat, I received a phone call from a woman who wanted to tell me about her husband's experience during the retreat. She recounted how she and her husband had gone there on Monday evening with their daughter who suffered from dyslexia. They wanted Sr Briege to pray for her.

'But when we got there,' she said, 'we discovered that Sr Briege would not be praying until the following evening. Anyway, we decided to go to Confession.'

She then went on to tell me that her husband, who had a paralysed leg because of polio, came to me for Confession. 'That night,' she said, 'when my husband was going to bed, he felt a strange and unusual tingling in his withered leg. The next morning he began to feel muscle growing in the leg and over the course of the next few days his leg was restored to normal. He no longer limps and does not need the brace that he has worn for most of his life.'

I have no doubt that Jesus performed this miracle to remind us all that He really is present and that He not only forgives our sins, but heals us spiritually, emotionally and physically.

On one occasion a country woman came to Confession one morning during a parish retreat. She wasn't sure whether to kneel behind the screen or come around and sit facing me. It was her first time in the new church. After a moment of hesitation, she came around and sat down in front of me.

'What do I do now?' she asked.

I said, 'Go ahead and make your Confession as usual.' So she went through the formula, 'Bless me, Father...' and told her sins, but with such great speed she was difficult to understand.

Not to embarrass her I said, 'I'm sorry. I was a bit distracted.'

She said, 'I'll start again, Father' and she spoke even faster the second time. At that, I raised my hand and said, 'How are you?'

She stopped and looked at me, 'To tell you the truth, Father, I'm not great.'

'What's the matter?' I said.

And she began to tell me about the poor health of her husband and difficulties with her children and many other things, the tears running down her poor little wrinkled face. When she had finished, she said, 'Will I make Confession now, Father?'

I said, 'I don't think so. You have told me enough.' I gave her absolution and said some prayers with her for all the things she had mentioned. She was one of the many people, especially women, whose lives are weighed down by the sins of others. Her own sins were nothing compared to the weight that other people's sins had placed on her shoulders.

By the time I had finished talking with her and praying with her, I could see how Christ Himself had come to her. She had experienced the forgiving and healing Christ. He had *healed her sins*. She knew it and I knew it. The circumstances of her confined life remained the same, but she was no longer the same. She had new strength, a new assurance of God's plan for every moment of her life. Her life had been one long act of loving others and giving herself for them. She spent little time worrying about herself.

I have been blessed to meet so many people like this holy woman who fill the world with goodness and spread everywhere the loving presence of Jesus. God doesn't just love; He is love. He doesn't just forgive; He is forgiveness. Jesus knows very well how often we need forgiveness. It must hurt Him when people refuse to come and be forgiven. Jesus says, 'Behold, I stand at the door and knock' (Revelation 3:20).

Everyone can open this door at any time and let the Lord come in. The key to re-entering the Church is the Sacrament of Reconciliation, a humble Confession. To those who enter, Christ will be there with His mercy and His forgiveness and His healing grace. In the Gospel of Luke, Jesus paints a picture of the loving mercy of our Heavenly Father in the *Parable of the Prodigal Son*:

> And he said, 'There was a man who had two sons; and the younger of them said to

his father, "Father, give me the share of property that falls to me." And he divided his living between them. Not many days later, the younger son gathered all he had and took his journey into a far country, and there he squandered his property in loose living. And when he had spent everything, a great famine arose in that country, and he began to be in want. So he went and joined himself to one of the citizens of that country, who sent him into his fields to feed swine. And he would gladly have fed on the pods that the swine ate; and no one gave him anything. But when he came to himself he said, 'How many of my father's hired servants have bread enough and to spare, but I perish here with hunger! I will arise and go to my father, and I will say to him, "Father, I have sinned against heaven and before you; I am no longer worthy to be called your son; treat me as one of your hired servants."' And he arose and came to his father.

'But while he was yet at a distance, his father saw him and had compassion and ran and embraced him and kissed him. And the son said to him, "Father, I have sinned against heaven and before you; I am no longer worthy to be called your son." But the father said to his servants, "Bring quickly the best robe, and put it on him; and put a ring on his hand, and shoes on his feet; and bring the fatted calf and kill it,

I Will Come Myself

and let us eat and make merry; for this my
son was dead, and is alive again; he was
lost, and is found.'"

(Luke 15:11-24)

In this parable of Jesus, the younger son acts like any
other foolish boy who thinks he knows what is best and
has no trouble ignoring parental advice. He is really
quite insulting to his father who nevertheless gives him
what he wants and lets him go. Sometimes fathers have
no option but to humour such a child and allow him to
flee the nest. Here the son runs with his new-found
freedom and is soon surrounded by pseudo friends who
latch onto him and help him spend his money. Not long
after, grim reality confronts him and he finds himself
with no money, no friends and no income. He ends up
feeding pigs, which for a Jew at that time is about as
low as he could sink. Suddenly it dawns on him what a
fool he has been. He is worse off than the lowest-paid
servant in his father's house. He repents, acknowledges
his fault and decides to do something about it. 'I will
arise and go to my father.' He prepares a little speech to
make when he meets his father. Meanwhile, the father
has been worrying about his foolish young son. Each
evening he looks down the dusty road hoping for his
return. Then one day it happens and the father runs to
embrace his foolish boy. The son makes his little
prepared speech, but the father is so excited on seeing
him and so busy ordering the best robe and a ring and
shoes, that he hardly hears a word.

The robe, the ring, the shoes and the banquet are all
symbols of new life. He is made clean and clothed in
the robe of forgiveness and penitence. He is restored to

his former dignity, symbolised by the ring, and is now no longer the cause of sadness and grief, but of joy for the entire household. And that is how it is for anyone who returns to the Church and to the family of God. He is drawn into the heart of Christ who knows the depths of the Father's love and forgiveness.

The healing of sin is the greatest and most needed healing of all; without it no other healing matters. No one, no matter how terrible a life he may think he has lived, should ever be afraid to come back to the Lord and seek mercy and forgiveness. The Lord knows that there are patterns of weakness and sin in everyone's life, like resentment and making rash judgements. We bring faults like these to Jesus in Confession and over time, little by little, His grace, His presence to us in the sacrament, along with our own efforts, will change us and turn resentment and rash judgement into forgiveness, tolerance and love. But we have to want this and ask for it. Conversion from sin is a process. It takes time.

In the Acts of the Apostles we read, Jesus 'went about doing good, and healing all that were oppressed by the devil' (Acts 10:38).

Jesus, who disappeared from the sight of the apostles at the Ascension, immediately reappeared in the sacraments of the Church. The Jesus who went about healing during His public ministry has not gone away. He is living, still with us, still healing. Jesus the healer continues to make Himself present in the Church through the ministry of priests in the Sacrament of the Anointing of the Sick. For a very long time it was regarded as the Sacrament of the Dying. Thankfully, since the Second Vatican Council, pastoral practice has brought it into much greater relevance as

I Will Come Myself

a sacrament of the sick, a sacrament of healing. In this sacrament, Jesus is present as the healing Christ and the forgiver of sins.

St James writes in his epistle:

> Is any among you sick? Let him call for the elders of the church, and let them pray over him, anointing him with oil in the name of the Lord; and the prayer of faith will save the sick man, and the Lord will raise him up; and if he has committed sins he will be forgiven.
>
> (James 5:14-15)

During my priestly life, the Holy Spirit has blessed me with a special awareness of the power of this sacrament to bring comfort and healing, and I have seen this power of Jesus perform miracles.

Years ago I was asked by a young mother to come and see her daughter who was suffering from hydrocephalus. I went and saw the two-year old child sitting in a playpen, helplessly uncoordinated. The mother informed me that the doctors had told her that nothing could be done; that the poor child would never be able to go to school or learn. She said, 'Someone told me, Father, that you pray for healing.'

I said, 'I do,' and explained to her about my faith in the Sacrament of the Anointing of the Sick and how Jesus becomes present through the prayer of the Church, the laying on of hands and the anointing with the oil of the sick. People who are sick and especially the parents of sick children have no difficulty in believing that Jesus can heal. My problem, as I tried to pray and anoint this child, was with my own faith. The situation seemed so completely hopeless for this poor girl. I doubted that she would ever get better. After the anointing and the prayer I left, telling this grateful mother, whose faith was a lot more fervent than my own, that I would continue to pray for her and her child.

About four years later I received a phone call from this same woman. She reminded me of my visit to her home. She said, 'You know, Father, from the moment that you anointed and prayed with my little daughter she began to improve to the point where today she is a normal six-year old child. The only problem is that she is still a bit overactive. I wonder if I could take her to see you and maybe you could give her a little blessing.'

Maybe I shouldn't have been amazed at hearing this, but I was even more so when I saw this beautiful little girl, so normal and so full of life. In spite of all my doubts, Jesus had healed her.

Once in Canada, I was taken to see a woman who was in the last stages of multiple sclerosis. She was a person who had been very active in her parish and who was greatly loved by everyone. I have made it a practice before ministering the Sacrament of the Anointing of the Sick to explain to people that it is not a blessing with Holy Oil, but one of the seven Sacraments of the Church. The regrettable truth is that people know very little about this sacrament. I always take time to instruct them that through the ministry of the priest, through the laying on of hands and the anointing with the Oil of the Sick and the prayer of the Church, Jesus Christ comes sacramentally to the sick person. It is very important for the one receiving the sacrament to be present to Christ through faith. During the anointing of this sick woman, while I was laying hands on her, she

I Will Come Myself

told me that she experienced power and heat pass through her body. Two days later on a Sunday morning, to the amazement of everyone, she walked unaided into the church for the eleven o'clock Mass. They all knew her and were aware of the extent of her illness.

Another woman, Alice Kennedy, had returned from the hospital so that she could die at home. She had cancer and had wasted away to nothing more than skin and bones. Her husband was there with their four little children. I spoke to the children.

I said, 'You know, I can do nothing to cure your mother, but Jesus who is with us can do everything. Do you believe this?'

The faith of children is always simple and direct. They believed every word I said. And so I prayed the ritual prayers of the Church, laid on hands and anointed this young mother. Again, the Lord Himself came in His healing mercy and from the moment she was anointed, she began to improve and made a complete recovery to health. Sometimes people say of a certain priest that he has a great healing ministry. Every priest, by virtue of his ordination, has the healing ministry of Christ Himself, especially when he celebrates the sacraments, and the Sacrament of the Sick in particular.

The very first time I witnessed the power of Jesus at work in the Sacrament of the Sick was while I was still a young priest in the mid-1960s in Nigeria before Vatican II. I had been giving a parish retreat in a very poor place and one morning after Mass as I was standing outside the little church talking to the people, a man came forward carrying a young boy wrapped in a blanket. From the reaction of the people standing around, I sensed that the boy was ill, near to death.

The father gently placed him on the ground at my feet and said, 'Father, please ask God to heal my son.'

No one had ever said anything like that to me in my life and I truly did not know how to react or what to do. Suddenly, as if inspired, I thought of the Anointing of the Sick. I produced my Roman Ritual and began to pray in Latin the prayers of the Sacrament of Extreme Unction, as it was then called. I anointed the child on the eyes, ears, nose, lips, hands and feet.

When I had finished, I got the people to pray and after a few minutes the man lifted his son from the ground and went home.

That evening as Mass was beginning there was a great commotion in the church with much clapping and praising God and beating of drums. At first I did not know what was happening, but I soon realised what it was about. The same man was standing there in front of me with a great wide smile on his face. He said, 'Look, Father, my child is better. You cured my son.'

He said many more things to me, but I heard none of them. That was the first time in my short experience of being a priest that anything like that had happened. I was deeply moved in my spirit by this sign that Jesus had given to these poor people and to a young Irish priest who badly needed it. '*I will come Myself* [and cure him]' (Matthew 8:7). Jesus Christ is risen from the dead. He is real and shows Himself to those who look for Him with eyes of faith.

The Church's understanding of this sacrament is well explained in this passage from the *Catechism of the Catholic Church*:

> Christ invites his disciples to follow him by taking up their cross in their turn. By

following him they acquire a new outlook on illness and the sick. Jesus associates them with his own life of poverty and service. He makes them share in his ministry of compassion and healing: 'So they went out and preached that men should repent. And they cast out many demons, and anointed with oil many that were sick and healed them.

(*CCC:* 1506)

Not everyone who receives the Anointing of the Sick will be healed, but everyone who is anointed will somehow encounter the healing Christ.

To get a more comprehensive idea of the effects of the sacrament it is good to look at the prayers contained in the Rite of the Sacrament. For example, in the Litany of the Anointing, the Church prays, 'Come and strengthen them through this holy anointing,' so strengthening and giving people the courage to continue and to unite their sufferings with those of Christ is one of the effects of this sacrament. The priest also prays, 'Free them from sin and all temptation.' We know that in certain circumstances where it is not possible for the sick person to celebrate the Sacrament of Reconciliation, their sins can be forgiven through the Anointing of the Sick. In the final prayers we ask the Father, 'that through this anointing, this person will find comfort in suffering.' We pray, 'When he [she] is afraid, give him [her] courage; when afflicted, give him [her] patience; when dejected, afford him [her] hope.' These are all graces that Jesus imparts through this sacrament. He brings comfort, He drives out fear and He gives people courage and patience. In another prayer we pray, 'Heal his [her] sickness; forgive his [her] sins, expel all afflictions of mind and body; mercifully restore him [her] to full health.' In all of these ways the sacramental Christ ministers to His poor sick members in this sacrament.

This is a prayer taken from the Byzantine Rite at the Anointing of the Sick:

> Holy Father, physician of souls and bodies, You sent Your only-begotten Son, our Lord Jesus Christ, to heal every infirmity and to deliver us from death. By this anointing heal your servant N. of the spiritual and bodily sickness which afflicts him [her], and restore his [her] health by the grace of your Christ, through the prayers of our most holy Lady, the Mother of God and ever-virgin Mary, and of all Your saints. For You, our God, are the fountain of healing, and to You we give glory, together with Your only begotten Son, and Your consubstantial Spirit, now and forever. Amen.

Of course, the Divine Physician does not confine His healing power to the sacraments. God gives to some the special charism of healing as a sign of the grace of the Risen Lord (Cf. *CCC*:1508). In my work with Sr Briege I have personally witnessed many healings: physical, emotional and spiritual.

Chapter 15
Whose Law?

> And behold, one came up to him, saying, 'Teacher, what good deed must I do, to have eternal life?' And he said to him, 'Why do you ask me about what is good? One there is who is good. If you would enter life, keep the commandments.' He said to him, 'Which?' And Jesus said, 'You shall not kill, You shall not steal, You shall not bear false witness, Honor your father and mother, and, You shall love your neighbour as yourself.'
>
> (Matthew 19:16-19)

Jesus is the Eternal Word of God, the only Begotten Son of the Father, the totality of divine revelation. The young man in Matthew 19 asks Jesus, 'What good deed must I do to enter eternal life?' The Lord leaves him in no doubt as to what he must do. 'If you would enter life, keep the commandments.' Since Moses received the commandments they have been the battleground of spiritual warfare. The powers of darkness have relentlessly attempted to subvert Christ's followers from obedience to God's law. That same spiritual warfare continues unabated in every generation, especially our own.

For years now the secular world has been telling people that there is no need for God, that we can be the masters of our own destiny. We have experienced the social and sexual revolution that promised so much and bore only the bitter fruits of drugs, abortion, AIDS, terrifying addictions and violence. Now, the headiness of the sixties and seventies has given us a world where people live in a darkness so profound that it is hardly any longer a place to live a human life. Despair, even of life itself, is everywhere and the grossest obscenity is accepted as normal.

The commandments of God form the foundation of all morality and are an expression of the natural law which God places in the heart of every human being.

The First Commandment forbids the worship of false gods. The false gods of our times are not much different from those of ages past. They involve power, riches, greed, sex, racism, pleasure seeking, spiritism and so forth. These are the kinds of things that people put before God. They dishonour and disrespect the sovereignty of God Almighty.

The Second Commandment, to respect the name of God, reminds me of a good friend of mine, a singer and musician, and a story he told of when he was touring with his band in Germany. He related that one morning they were standing outside their hotel waiting for a taxi, and a German man who was standing nearby came over to them and said, 'You must be from Ireland. Are you?'

'Yes, how do you know?'

The man said, 'Only Irish people abuse the holy name of Jesus the way you have been doing.' And he walked away.

But it is not just the Irish who disrespect the name of God or call on God to witness their lies. 'Hallowed be Thy name,' we pray in the Our Father. May Your name be held holy.

The Third Commandment about keeping holy the Lord's day is being largely ignored by the modern world and Sunday has become like any other business day. For Catholics it is a day when we come together to give worship to the Father, through the celebration of the Mass, the Paschal Mystery, the Eucharistic sacrifice of Christ. It is our weekend invitation from Jesus to come and listen to Him speak and receive Him in Holy Communion. Jesus takes this invitation seriously and never fails to show up and is never late. We should respond in the same way. In receiving Jesus in the Eucharist, we receive all others in the unity of His love. Pope Benedict writes in his Apostolic Exhortation:

> Participating in the Sunday liturgical assembly with all our brothers and sisters, with whom we form one body in Jesus Christ, is demanded by our Christian conscience and at the same time it forms that conscience. To lose a sense of Sunday as the Lord's Day, a day to be sanctified, is symptomatic of the loss of an authentic sense of Christian freedom, the freedom of the children of God. Here some observations made by my venerable predecessor John Paul II in his Apostolic

Letter *Dies Domini* continue to have great value. Speaking of the various dimensions of the Christian celebration of Sunday, he said that it is *Dies Domini* (Lord's Day) with regard to the work of creation, *Dies Christi* (Christ's Day) as the day of the new creation and the Risen Lord's gift of the Holy Spirit, *Dies Ecclesiae* (Church's Day) as the day on which the Christian community gathers for the celebration, and *Dies Hominis* (Man's Day) as the day of joy, rest and fraternal charity. Sunday thus appears as the primordial holy day.

(*Sacramentum Caritatis*. 73)

The Fourth Commandment says, 'Honor your father and your mother.' We read in Deuteronomy 5:16: 'Honor your father and your mother as the Lord your God commanded you, that your days may be prolonged and that it may go well with you.' Children who honour and obey their parents are blessed by God. Today many parents fail to care for their children. God blesses parents with children and He expects that they form them and bring them up to know and obey God and to live good lives. But many no longer bother to do this. They take no part in the religious and spiritual formation of their offspring and give them no instruction in how to pray and no example of how to live Godly and religious lives.

Blessed Teresa of Calcutta once said, 'One of the worst forms of child neglect is not to tell them about God.' Parents should remember that one day they will have to answer to God concerning their failure to

I Will Come Myself

instruct their children in the ways of goodness that will lead them to Eternal Life.

The Fifth Commandment covers all the issues relating to human life which are of such enormous importance to modern man. Human life is a gift that comes directly from the creative hand of God. It places us in a unique relationship with our Heavenly Father from whom we have come and to whom we shall return. God is the Lord of life from its beginning to its natural end and no human authority can arrogate this power of God.

Modern science has discovered much which directly threatens the culture of life. The fact remains that every human person, whether he be ten-minutes old or a hundred-years old, has this right to life that no one may take from him. God gives life and God alone has the right to take it away. So, however young or old a person may be, no one has any right to end his or her life. Most people have little difficulty with the more solemn aspects of this commandment.

Some women cite the right to privacy as giving them a kind of sovereignty over their bodies and as a consequence, the right to choose to have an abortion. Not long ago men said that the right to private property was to be upheld in relation to slave ownership. No one would dare to make such a claim today because there is no right to private property which could ever conceivably take precedence over a human being's right to freedom. This is even truer of the right to life. There is not, nor ever could be, any right to privacy or any right to choose that could come before a person's right to life. There are many hypocritical utterances and laws in this world, but none that can equal the one that tries to justify the gruesome practice of abortion. How any nation or civilised people could allow legalised abortion is beyond belief. The human person comes into existence at the moment of conception. The womb is the place of God's exclusive work of creation where only the healing hand may enter. Abortion, as well as being a sin against God's Fifth Commandment, is an even more serious sin against His divine majesty, an affront, an insult to God the creator.

Modern society has created the abortion mentality and the culture of death that goes with it. Today young people have accepted abortion as something normal. They don't think much about it, that is, until they go through the experience, which is truly devastating. It has been said that there are always two victims in abortion – the child and the mother. Some years ago a woman came to me during a parish retreat. She said, 'You remember me, Father, from yesterday when I spoke to you? I came because I wanted to find out if you were the sort of priest I could talk to. You see, thirty years ago I had an abortion and I didn't want to go to Confession without knowing whether you would forgive me or not.' I immediately reassured her.

'All these years,' she said, 'I have lived in hell thinking that the Church would not have me back.' I asked her to go home and read the Parable of the Prodigal Son (Cf. Luke 15:11-24) and come for Confession the following day. She agreed to that.

I learned from her how important it is for priests to reach out to such suffering souls. Their grief is heartbreaking; their remorse is crippling. Priests, especially in these times, need to give an indication that they are 'the sort of priest' that such women can come to. These women already feel condemned enough without receiving more condemnation from the altar.

It is commonly thought that a child conceived because of rape should be aborted; that a woman has the right to terminate the life of a child conceived in this way. Sometimes such a child is portrayed as an aggressor. One mystic, writing on this topic, received a revelation from the Lord. She wrote that such a child, far from being an aggressor, is intended to be a blessing and a consolation from God to compensate for the awful experience of being raped. From time to time I have seen on television a mother and a daughter whom she conceived through rape. Usually such people are involved in the pro-life movement. No right, no matter how legal, supersedes the right to life. Every human life is sacred.

Euthanasia is one of the issues of the day and it is amazing how easily and thoughtlessly so many have come to accept it. My brother died after a battle with an unusual form of cancer which caused him great suffering and pain. In the end, he would have seemed in the eyes of some to be a perfect candidate for euthanasia. It could have been said, 'He has no quality of life. Why prolong his suffering?' Externally it might have appeared that he had a poor quality of life. But he had another life, an interior life of grace through which he united himself and every moment of his suffering to Christ on the Cross. He had a very clear understanding of the value of redemptive suffering. He believed firmly that not one moment of his pain would be wasted and that as he united his suffering to that of Christ on the Cross, he was helping many to come to salvation. He knew about reparation and about making up 'what is lacking in Christ's afflictions' (Colossians 1:24) and he embraced it.

I used to watch him at Mass after he had received Holy Communion. In spite of all of his pain, I could see how closely he was united to Christ in prayer. As a disciple of Jesus Christ, his life was of a very high quality indeed. God is the Divine Artist who knows when and where the final brush strokes should be painted. No one should ever presume that He has finished.

As for suicide, is God's mercy absent from such souls? It could happen that a person might commit suicide out of hatred for God or for some other contumacious reason. Usually people who take their own lives do so not because they hate God or the commandments or the Church or their family. No, they choose to end their lives because of some deep suffering. Ill-will towards anyone is hardly ever involved.

God's mercy is never absent from such souls. Many feel great grief and helplessness. They suffer greatly under the weight of heavy crosses of sickness or addiction, anxiety, loneliness or rejection. They look at the future and see only more of the same. In the midst of all this they lose true perspective and balance in their lives. They forget that God is near, that Jesus is there for them. But the Lord does not forget them. He is close to them at their last moment in this life and in the first moments of the life to come. We pray that Jesus will be the first One they will encounter with His embrace of mercy and forgiveness. We hope that they will run to Him and that He will receive them. Family members, especially parents, should comfort themselves with this thought. They should pray and have Masses offered for their child that he [or she] may be cleansed in the blood of Christ and brought to the happiness and joy of eternal life.

The Sixth and Ninth Commandments which forbid adultery and the destruction of Christian marriage are two of the commandments that some people think disappeared after Vatican II, or so they would like to believe. Is adultery a sin? Yes, it is. Is it a serious sin? Yes, it is, because it violates one of the most solemn covenants that can exist between two human beings: 'I take you ... till death do us part ...' 'Every one who looks at a woman lustfully has already committed adultery with her in his heart' (Matthew 5:28).

The sexual revolution of the 1960s and the 1970s has done great damage to marriage and to family life. Many today think that if things don't work out, they can just walk away, Hollywood-style, and start over with somebody else. Any couple who has been married for a while will tell you that to make a marriage last requires great effort and much grace.

Our fallen nature has left us prone to every kind of sin and disorder, especially in the area of sexuality. This is denied in the world of today, where the so-called right to sexual expression reigns supreme over all else. It seems that nothing must be said or done to impinge upon this sexual freedom. The sexual revolution was greatly facilitated by the discovery of chemical contraception.

Pope Paul VI's worst fears in the aftermath of the publication of *Humanae Vitae* have unfortunately been realised. In the past the Church was accused of being preoccupied with sex. If that was true then, it is no longer so. Today the pulpits are often silent about sins of the flesh. So, is it sinful for people to have sex outside of marriage? Yes, it is. And it is wrong for cohabiting couples to claim the same right to receive the Eucharist as married people.

St Paul, in his Letter to the Galatians, contrasts the works of the flesh with those of the Spirit:

> But I say, walk by the Spirit, and do not gratify the desires of the flesh. For the desires of the flesh are against the Spirit, and the desires of the Spirit are against the flesh; for these are opposed to each other, to prevent you from doing what you would. But if you are led by the Spirit you are not under the law. Now the works of the flesh are plain: immorality, impurity, licentiousness, idolatry, sorcery, enmity, strife, jealousy, anger, selfishness, dissension, party spirit, envy, drunkenness, carousing, and the like. I warn you, as I warned you before, that those who do such things shall not inherit the kingdom of God. But the fruit of the Spirit is love, joy, peace, patience, kindness, goodness, faithfulness, gentleness, self-control; against such there is no law. And those who belong to Christ Jesus have crucified the flesh with its passions and desires. If we live by the Spirit, let us also walk by the Spirit. Let us have no self-conceit, no provoking of one another, no envy of one another.
>
> (Galatians 5:16-26)

And the same St Paul lifts us up in the midst of all these struggles with words of encouragement in his Letter to the Romans:

> So then, brethren, we are debtors, not to the flesh, to live according to the flesh – for if you live according to the flesh you will die, but if by the Spirit you put to death the deeds of the body, you will live. For all who are led by the Spirit of God are sons of God. For you did not receive the spirit of slavery to fall back into fear, but you have received the spirit of sonship. When we cry, 'Abba! Father!' it is the Spirit himself bearing witness with our spirit that we are children of God, and if children, then heirs, heirs of God and fellow heirs with Christ, provided we suffer with him in order that we may also be glorified with him.
>
> (Romans 8:12-17)

The Seventh Commandment states, 'Thou shall not steal' and forbids the taking and keeping of what belongs to other people. It also forbids the destruction of other people's property. This commandment is the basis and foundation of the Church's social teaching on justice and charity, and everything pertaining to the fruits of man's work and the goods and fruits of the earth. St James in his letter writes:

> Come now, you rich, weep and howl for the miseries that are coming upon you.

Your riches have rotted and your garments are moth-eaten. Your gold and silver have rusted, and their rust will be evidence against you and will eat your flesh like fire. You have laid up treasure for the last days. Behold, the wages of the labourers who mowed your fields, which you kept back by fraud, cry out; and the cries of the harvesters have reached the ears of the Lord of hosts. You have lived on the earth in luxury and in pleasure; you have fattened your hearts in a day of slaughter. You have condemned; you have killed the righteous man; he does not resist you.

(James 5:1-6)

The Tenth Commandment is connected to the Seventh Commandment. Again, to quote the *Catechism of the Catholic Church*:

You shall not covet ... anything that is your neighbour's. You shall not desire your neighbour's house, his field, or his manservant, or his maidservant, or his ox, or his ass, or anything that is your neighbour's. For where your treasure is, there will your heart be also.

(Deuteronomy 5:12)
(Matthew 6:21)
(*CCC*: 2534)

Blessed Teresa of Calcutta died leaving one worn-out habit and a plastic bucket. Pope John Paul II died possessing nothing.

I Will Come Myself

The eighth commandment forbids misrepresenting the truth in our relations with others. This moral prescription flows from the vocation of the holy people to bear witnes to their God who is the truth and wills the truth. Offences against the truth express by word or deed a refusal to commit oneself to moral uprightness: they are fundamental infidelities to God and, in this sense, they undermine the foundations of the covenant.

(*CCC*: 2464)

Many think nothing of lying. They even invoke God to witness that their lies are the truth. They swear on the Bible to tell the truth, the whole truth and nothing but the truth; and proceed to tell lies, total lies and nothing but lies. God is greatly offended by this. St James, who was not a man to mince words, writes:

> So the tongue is a little member and boasts of great things. How great a forest is set ablaze by a small fire! And the tongue is a fire. The tongue is an unrighteous world among our members, staining the whole body, setting on fire the cycle of nature, and set on fire by hell. For every kind of beast and bird, of reptile and sea creature, can be tamed and has been tamed by mankind, but no human being can tame the tongue – a restless evil, full of deadly poison. With it we bless the Lord and Father, and with it we curse men, who are made in the likeness of God. From the

same mouth come blessing and cursing. My brethren, this ought not to be so. Does a spring pour forth from the same opening fresh water and brackish? Can a fig tree, my brethren, yield olives, or a grapevine, figs? No more can salt water yield fresh. Who is wise and understanding among you? By his good life let him show his works in the meekness of wisdom. But if you have bitter jealousy and selfish ambition in your hearts, do not boast and be false to the truth. This wisdom is not such as comes down from above, but is earthly, unspiritual, devilish. For where jealousy and selfish ambition exist, there will be disorder and every vile practice. But the wisdom from above is first pure, then peaceable, gentle, open to reason, full of mercy and good fruits, without uncertainty or insincerity. And the harvest of righteousness is sown in peace by those who make peace.

(James 3:5-18)

There is a short prayer that I say frequently which reads: 'Heavenly Father, protect Your perfect plan for my life and let nothing interfere with it.' God has a perfect plan for everyone's life and His commandments are an integral part of it. We can live our lives in obedience to God or we can choose to go our own way. The baptised person is one who lives with the life of Jesus, who said, 'I am the way, and the truth, and the life' (John 14:6).

I Will Come Myself

One of the psalms gives expression to how we should embrace God's law:

> The law of the Lord is perfect,
> reviving the soul;
> the testimony of the Lord is sure,
> making wise the simple;
> the precepts of the Lord are right,
> rejoicing the heart;
> the commandment of the Lord is pure,
> enlightening the eyes;
> the fear of the Lord is clean,
> enduring for ever;
> the ordinances of the Lord are true,
> and the righteous altogether.
> More to be desired are they than gold,
> even much fine gold;
> sweeter also than honey
> and drippings of the honeycomb.
> Moreover by them is thy servant warned;
> in keeping them there is great reward.
> But who can discern his errors?
> Clear thou me from hidden faults.
> Keep back thy servant also from
> presumptuous sins;
> let them not have dominion over me!
> Then I shall be blameless,
> and innocent of great transgression.
> Let the words of my mouth and the
> meditation of my heart
> be acceptable in thy sight,
> O Lord, my rock and my redeemer
>
> (Psalm 19:7-14)

Chapter 16
Flame of Divine Love

The foundation of the edifice of the Church is the Sacraments of Initiation – Baptism, Confirmation and Eucharist. Christ comes to live within us; it is no longer we who live, but Christ who lives in us (Cf. Galatians 2:20). The life of Baptism is made strong by Confirmation and the manifold gifts of the Holy Spirit. It is nourished by Jesus, the Bread of Life, in the Holy Eucharist.

Through the action of the Holy Spirit, we understand what Baptism does to the soul – that through it we are born again into new life in Christ, that Original Sin is forgiven along with all other sins, that we become children of the Father, that we recognise Jesus as our Saviour and our brother, and that we are made holy by the presence and love of the Holy Spirit. We literally become temples of the Holy Trinity. What a pity that so many people do not have a clearer understanding of what Baptism does. It does make us children of God; it transforms our soul and marks it with a character, an irreversible uniqueness which lasts into eternity. Once baptised, always baptised.

Baptism forgives and undoes the fault of Adam and Eve which we call Original Sin, that fatal flaw inherited by every human being. Adam and Eve, when tempted by Satan, preferred themselves to God. They trusted Satan rather than God. God said, 'Do not eat' and Satan said 'Eat' and they ate. God said 'Obey' and Satan said 'Disobey' and they disobeyed and lost their innocence, their peace and their place in Paradise, not just for themselves but for all of us. It was to reverse this tragedy that Jesus came into the world. Judging by the price Jesus paid on the Cross, the sin of Adam and Eve must have been very serious indeed.

St Paul put it this way, 'Then as one man's trespass led to condemnation for all men, so one man's act of righteousness leads to acquittal and life for all men. For by one man's disobedience many were made sinners, so by one man's obedience many will be made righteous' (Romans 5:18-19).

I often wonder as I baptise their children if parents realise the seriousness of the duty they undertake. Do they realise that the God who gives them children will also hold them responsible for how they have instructed their children and taught them to follow Christ and to walk in the ways of righteousness? God's plan is that every child become a saint. Parents must help their children to hear God's word and to live out their Baptismal promises to reject Satan and his ways, and to always be open to the Spirit who comes in power at Confirmation.

The restored Rite of Christian Initiation makes it very clear that when people are being prepared for these foundational sacraments, they should be instructed with such thoroughness that it will influence their entire Christian lives, as well as initiating them into the Mystery of Salvation.

They should learn how to live according to Gospel values and be instructed in the ways of faith and charity. New Christians should be aware that the Eucharistic liturgy is the great meeting point of God's people. They should know about the sacraments and that these infallible encounters with Jesus Christ are the very life of the Church, the Body of Christ.

Normally people rely on Catholic schools, religious education programs or the Rite of Christian Initiation for Adults to prepare them to live their faith and face up to the tasks before them as Catholics. Unfortunately, experience has shown that this is not always so and that many children grow up either having been taught badly or not at all. The Rite of Baptism reminds parents that they are to be the 'first and best teachers of their children in the ways of faith'.

Personally, I learned more about prayer from the family Rosary than I did anywhere else. The same is true about repentance, from seeing my mother and father go to Confession and making sure that we children did the same. Parental witness is the best teacher of all. As a child, I watched my mother welcome a poor travelling woman and her child into our home, sitting them down at the table and giving them a meal. My mother never said anything to me about being kind to the poor or seeing Christ in them; she did not need to.

Today parents have to keep guard over their children and not abandon them to be formed by the influences of the secular world. Parents have a moral duty to teach their children, protect their innocence,

I Will Come Myself

and instruct them in Christian moral values. In earlier times young people absorbed such values from the communities in which they grew up. Sadly this is no longer the case.

Why is Baptism so important? It is important because it is the foundation stone of the Christian life. It is the most important of all the sacraments, because it gives us a share in the life and mysteries of Jesus Christ. Baptised people belong no longer to themselves, but to God. Like Jesus they are called to be servants, to profess their faith openly, to be part of the Church's mission, to establish God's Kingdom on earth. At Baptism they begin a life of discipleship, following and obeying the Gospel of Jesus Christ proclaimed by the Church, even to the shedding of their blood.

Confirmation is the second Sacrament of Christian Initiation and in it the Father and the Son send the Holy Spirit uniquely and infallibly into the soul of the baptised person. Confirmation continues and completes the mission of the Holy Spirit which began at Baptism. The grace of the Holy Spirit helps the person to take on the responsibilities of loving service to God and neighbour.

In the Rite of Confirmation the Bishop prays for an outpouring of the gifts of the Holy Spirit received in Baptism. The effect of this sacrament is a special outpouring of the Holy Spirit like that granted to the apostles on the day of Pentecost. Confirmation imparts an increase and deepening of the grace of Baptism. It makes us more aware that we are children of God and causes us to cry out, 'Abba! Father!' (Romans 8:15). It unites us more firmly with Christ; it increases the gifts of the Holy Spirit within us, and makes us more perfect members of the Church. Confirmation also gives us a special strength of the Holy Spirit to witness to and defend the faith by word and action, and helps us to confess the name of Jesus Christ boldly without fear or shame. St Ambrose wrote,

> Recall then that you have received the spiritual seal, the spirit of wisdom and understanding, the spirit of right judgement and courage, the spirit of knowledge and reverence, the spirit of holy fear in God's presence. Guard what you have received. God the Father has marked you with his sign; Christ the Lord has confirmed you and has placed his pledge, the Spirit, in your hearts.
>
> (St Ambrose, *De Myst*)
> (*CCC*: 1303)

Where do saintly people get their wisdom, their capacity to understand the unfathomable trials of life? It is given to them by the Holy Sprit. The same is true of their indomitable courage, their sincere piety, their great reverence for God and for the things of God. St Ambrose writes of the martyr St Agnes:

> Today is the birthday of St Agnes who is said to have suffered martyrdom at the age of twelve. The cruelty that did not spare her youth shows all the more clearly the power of faith in finding one so young to bear it witness. There was little or no room

in that small body for a wound. Though she could scarcely receive the blow, she could rise superior to it. Girls of her age cannot bear even their parents' frowns and, pricked by a needle, weep as for a serious wound. Yet she shows no fear of the bloodstained hands of her executioners. She stands undaunted by heavy, clanking chains. She offers her whole body to be put to the sword by fierce soldiers. She is too young to know of death, yet is ready to face it. Dragged against her will to the altars, she stretches out her hands to the Lord in the midst of the flames, making the triumphant sign of Christ the victor on the altars of sacrilege. She puts her neck and hands in iron chains, but no chain can hold fast her tiny limbs.

A new kind of martyrdom! Too young to be punished, yet old enough for a martyr's crown; unfitted for the contest, yet effortless in victory, she shows herself a master in valour despite the handicap of youth.

(*Office of Readings*: 21 January,
Feast of St Agnes)

What gives a twelve-year old girl such fortitude? It is the Holy Spirit who helps her and strengthens her at that moment. Similarly with St Maria Goretti and a host of martyrs, young and old, who have laid down their lives for Jesus Christ. It is the same with mothers and fathers who 'suffer the heartache and the thousand natural shocks that flesh is heir to' to provide for their families. And where does the young Chinese priest or the old Chinese bishop find the courage to persevere over years of cruel imprisonment? All this is the work of the Holy Spirit in the Sacrament of Confirmation. It is like a personal Pentecost which causes us to grow in the grace of our Baptism. It too, like Baptism, leaves a *permanent character* – an imprint on the soul. It strengthens us as children of the Father and binds us firmly to Jesus Christ and the Church. It enlivens us with the gifts of the Holy Spirit. The Sacrament of Confirmation embraces every facet of our Christian lives.

In my own life I have often needed to call on the help of the Holy Spirit in preaching the word of God. One incident in particular stands out in my mind. It concerned a young Korean priest who was attending the conference where Sr Briege and I were the main speakers. It was a weekend for Korean Catholics living in the United States. I was delighted on the morning of Trinity Sunday when he came to me and said, 'Father Kevin, I will give the homily at the Mass.' I shouldn't have been so pleased, but I was. Explaining the mystery of the Trinity to people has never been one of my great achievements. I came to the Eucharist in a relaxed mood, glad to be able to sit back and listen to the homily, rather than having to preach it.

During the second reading one of the leaders went over to the young priest and whispered something in his ear. He then leaned over to me and said, 'Fr Kevin, you will preach the homily.'

I said, 'But, I thought you were doing it.'

'No,' he said, 'you must do it.'

Now I have often been on the spot regarding homilies, when I had little time to prepare. This, however, was different because I hadn't thought of even the possibility of having to preach. When the Gospel was being proclaimed I remember praying to the Holy Spirit and saying, 'Holy Spirit, You know how much and how often I have needed You in the past. Now I need You desperately. Please help me.' This prayer was on my lips as I walked over to preach the homily. I never found out what anyone thought of my homily, but I was so impressed with what I was saying that I thought to myself, wouldn't I love to be listening to this homily? What I experienced of the help of the Holy Spirit at that moment was very real to me. The Spirit helped me when I called out to Him in my time of need.

On 30 May 1998, Pope John Paul II held an unprecedented and historical meeting with the members of the ecclesial movements and new communities from around the world. The address he gave in St Peters Square that Saturday contained the most sublime teaching on the work of the Holy Spirit. I could do no better than to quote from this inspired address:

> The Holy Spirit, already at work in the creation of the world and in the Old Covenant, reveals himself in the incarnation and the Paschal Mystery of the Son of God, and in a way 'bursts out' at Pentecost to extend the mission of Christ the Lord in time and space. The Spirit thus makes the Church a stream of new life that flows through the history of mankind ...
>
> Whenever the Spirit intervenes He leaves people astonished. He brings about events of amazing newness; He radically changes

persons and history. This was the unforgettable experience of the Second Vatican Ecumenical Council during which, under the guidance of the Spirit, the Church rediscovered Her charismatic dimension.

Here the Holy Father quotes from the Dogmatic Constitution of the Church: *Lumen Gentium* XII:

> It is not only through the Sacraments and the ministries of the Church that the Holy Spirit makes holy the people, leads them and enriches them with His virtues. Allotting His gifts according as He wills, He also distributes special graces among the faithful of every rank ... He makes them fit and ready to undertake various tasks and offices for the renewal and building up of the Church.

A Dogmatic Constitution is a solemn declaration of the faith of the whole Church, and a solemn teaching of the Magisterium.

The Pope then took the teaching of the Second Vatican Council a stage further when he said:

> The institutional and charismatic aspects [of the Church] are co-essential, as it were, to the Church's constitution. They contribute, although differently, to the life, renewal and sanctification of the Church.

When the Pope said that institutional and charismatic aspects were co-essential, he meant that they are of equal importance, though they contribute to the life of the Church in different ways. In the recent past we have seen two magnificent examples of both these facets of the Church's life in the persons of Pope John Paul II from the institutional Church and Blessed Teresa of Calcutta from the charismatic side. The Pope went on to say:

> This providential recovery of the Church's charismatic dimension both before and after the Council has proved a remarkable pattern of growth for the ecclesial movements and new communities.
>
> Today the Church rejoices at the renewed confirmation of the words of the Prophet Joel, 'I will pour out my spirit on all flesh.' Your presence here is the tangible proof of this outpouring of the Holy Spirit. Each renewal movement is different from the others, but they are all united in the same communion and for the same mission. Some charisms given by the Spirit blow like an impetuous wind. This wind seizes people and carries them to new ways of missionary commitment to the radical service of the Gospel. They become zealous in ceaselessly proclaiming the truths of faith; they accept the living stream of tradition as a gift which instills in each person a real desire for holiness.
>
> Today, I would like to cry out to all of you gathered in St Peters Square and to all Christians. Open yourselves docilely to the gifts of the Spirit. Accept gratefully and

obediently the charisms which the Spirit never ceases to bestow on us. Do not forget that every charism is given for the common good, that is, for the benefit of the whole Church.

The Pope went on to give a remarkable teaching about the true function of the charisms of the Holy Spirit:

True charisms can not but aim at the encounter with Christ in the Sacraments. The ecclesial realities to which you belong have helped you to rediscover your Baptismal vocation, to appreciate the gifts of the Spirit received at Confirmation, to entrust yourselves to God's forgiveness in the Sacrament of Reconciliation and to recognise the Eucharist as the source and the summit of all Christian life. Thanks to this powerful ecclesial experience, wonderful Christian families have come into being which are open to life, and true domestic churches and many vocations to the ministerial priesthood and the religious life have blossomed, as well as new forms of lay life inspired by the evangelical council. You have learned in the movements and new communities that faith is not abstract talk nor vague religious sentiments, but new life in Christ instilled by the Holy Spirit.

(Pope John Paul II, Papal Address,
30 May 1998)

It is the will of the Father that every action of Jesus in the Church on earth is done by the power of the Holy Spirit, even at the celebration of the Eucharist, when bread and wine become the Body and Blood of Christ. In the third Eucharistic Prayer, the priest prays, 'And so, Father, we bring You these gifts. We ask You to make them holy by the power of the Spirit, that they may become the Body and Blood of Your Son, Jesus Christ.' Nothing good happens in the Church that is not the work of the Holy Spirit. Nothing good happens in the soul of a baptised person unless by the power of the Holy Spirit. Indeed, nothing happens in the created universe unless through the power of the Spirit.

In St John's Gospel, Jesus said,

> I have yet many things to say to you, but you cannot bear them now. When the Spirit of truth comes, he will guide you into all the truth; for he will not speak on his own authority, but whatever he hears he will speak, and he will declare to you the things that are to come.
>
> (John 16:12-13)

More than ever we need the help and gifts of the Holy Spirit to discern the signs of the times and the spirit of the age. The Church is engaged in intense spiritual warfare. In our own time people are saying we do not need a saviour from outside the human experience; that human beings are well able to control their own destiny. On 29 November 1972 in a general audience, Pope Paul VI spoke about the need for the Church to be guided by the Holy Spirit. I quote:

I have asked myself on several occasions what are the greatest needs of the Church ... [The Church needs]: the Spirit, the Holy Spirit, the animator and sanctifier ... her divine breath ... her unifying principle, her inner source of light and strength, her support and consoler, her source of charisms and songs, her peace and her joy .... The Church needs her perennial Pentecost; she needs fire in the heart, words on the lips, prophecy in the glance. The Church needs to be the temple of the Holy Spirit .... She needs to feel within her, in the silent emptiness of us modern men, all turned outwards because of the spell of exterior life, charming, fascinating, corrupting with delusions of false happiness, [she needs] to feel rising from the depths of her inmost personality ... the praying voice of the Spirit who, as St Paul teaches us, takes our place and prays in us and for us 'with sighs too deep for words,' and who interprets the words that we by ourselves would not be able to address to God ... Living men, you young people, and you consecrated souls, you brothers in the priesthood, are you listening to me? This is what the Church needs. She needs the Holy Spirit. The Holy Spirit in us, in each of us, and in all of us together, in us who are the Church ... So let all of you ever say to him 'Come!'.

(Pope Paul VI, General Audience,
29 November 1972)

I Will Come Myself

Many people, even theologians, simply do not know what the Spirit is saying to the Church, because they do not take time to pray and allow the Holy Spirit to act upon them. Those who live in the world of God and the Church must pray for the enlightenment of the Holy Spirit. If they do not, they quickly lose touch with reality. So many mistakes have been made, even by religious people, because they did not invoke the help of the Holy Spirit. Think of the disintegration of religious life that has taken place in the last thirty years. Instead of returning to the charism of their founder and to the well-springs of living faith that sprang up from there, many have gone in the opposite direction. When you read about a group of religious performing a druidic ritual dance on the top of an Irish mountain, you can be sure that they are not being led by the Spirit of the living God. 'He will teach you all things' (John 14:26); that is the guarantee that Jesus gives us if we are willing to learn.

The hymn *Veni Sancte Spiritus*, which is known as the 'golden sequence', provides us with a poetic description of the activity of the Holy Spirit in the lives of the faithful. It has a beauty and depth that is greatly enhanced by the plain chant music to which it is sung. No one actually knows who wrote it, but it has been attributed to Stephen Langton, who was Archbishop of Canterbury in the beginning of the thirteenth century. Even in translation it is a sublime prayer invoking the Holy Spirit:

> Come, Holy Spirit, come!
> And from your celestial home
> Shed a ray of light divine!

Come, Father of the poor!
Come, source of all our store!
Come, within our bosoms shine.
You, of comforters the best;
You, the soul's most welcome guest;
Sweet refreshment here below;
In our labour, rest most sweet;
Grateful coolness in the heat;
Solace in the midst of woe.
O most blessed Light divine,
Shine within these hearts of yours
And our inmost being fill!
Where you are not, we have naught,
Nothing good in deed or thought,
Nothing free from taint of ill.
Heal our wounds, our strength renew;
On our dryness pour your dew;
Wash the stains of guilt away;
Bend the stubborn heart and will;
Melt the frozen, warm the chill;
Guide the steps that go astray
On the faithful, who adore
And confess you, evermore
In your sevenfold gift descend;
Give them virtue's sure reward;
Give them your salvation, Lord;
Give them joys that never end.

Chapter 17
Sexuality, the Divine Gift

> So God created man in his own image, in
> the image of God he created him; male and
> female he created them.
>
> (Genesis 1:27)

Sexual freedom is the great 'sacred cow' of this present
age and no one dares to question people's right to such
freedom. Hollywood and the visual media must share
some of the blame for the almost total absence of any
kind of chastity or sexual self-restraint so widespread in
the sexual culture of our time. I once asked a twenty-
something year old woman in Ireland why it was that
so many young Irish people were turning away from
their Catholic faith. Without a moment's hesitation she
said, 'Sex, Father. They are destroying their faith
because of their sexual activity.'

Her answer came as no surprise to me, though
coming so directly from one of her generation did
surprise me. In our own time sex has been debased to
just a tool of human pleasure, even in some parts of the
world a tourist attraction. The availability of physical
and chemical contraception has reduced human

sexuality to a grossness never before imagined. Add to that the widespread acceptance of pornography, and its devastating effects on the innocence of young people, and you have a world so dark that it seems no longer a fit place to rear children.

There are few areas of human life in which the presence of the healing Christ is more needed than that of human sexuality. Today a great deception has been foisted on human beings. People are being told that sex and sexuality are to be sought and enjoyed as a kind of absolute right without any consequence or responsibility. This great lie has caused much pain and suffering and has brought darkness and ugliness into society. The healing of this pain and the dispelling of this darkness can only be found by seeking the experience of the Risen Christ in their lives so that people, especially the young, will come to the realisation of the unique beauty of their sexuality.

Pope Benedict XVI writes:

> The contemporary way of exalting the body is deceptive. *Eros*, reduced to pure 'sex' has become a commodity, a mere 'thing' to be bought and sold, or rather, man himself becomes a commodity. This is hardly man's great 'yes' to the body. On the contrary, he now considers his body and his sexuality as the purely material part of himself, to be used and exploited at will. Nor does he see it as an arena for the exercise of his freedom, but as a mere object that he attempts, as he pleases, to make both enjoyable and harmless. Here

we are actually dealing with a debasement of the human body: no longer is it integrated into our overall existential freedom; no longer is it a vital expression of our whole being, but it is more or less relegated to the purely biological sphere. The apparent exaltation of the body can quickly turn into a hatred of bodiliness. Christian faith, on the other hand, has always considered man a unity in duality, a reality in which spirit and matter compenetrate, and in which each is brought to a new nobility. True *eros* tends to rise 'in ecstasy' towards the Divine, to lead us beyond ourselves; yet for this very reason it calls for a path of ascent, renunciation, purification, and healing.

(*Deus Caritas Est*: 5)

When God created human beings He created them in His own image, 'male and female he created them' (Genesis 1:27). Being in God's image, they were spiritual and immortal, as well as physical. Their physical bodies reflected the divinity in their beauty and complementarity. 'God fashioned man with his own hands [that is, the Son and the Holy Spirit] and impressed his own form on the flesh he had fashioned, in such a way that even what was visible might bear the divine form' (*CCC*: 704). They were destined to live in Paradise, in a state of innocence where they experienced nothing of sin. Then God gave them obedience concerning 'the forbidden fruit' (Cf. Genesis 2:16). When they failed this obedience, they forfeited their place in Paradise and instead of experiencing the freedom and physical compatibility of their bodies, they began to experience guilt and shame. So what was most beautiful and Godlike in their nature, their capacity to love and give life, became for them a source of great difficulty and struggle.

This shadow of guilt and shame has hung over men and women down the ages. The body, instead of being the human expression of God's love and life, became flawed and open to every kind of selfishness. Christ, the Son of Mary, the New Eve, through the blood of His Cross has redeemed every part of our fallen humanity, especially human sexuality. St Paul speaks of this in his letter to the Romans:

> Let not sin therefore reign in your mortal bodies, to make you obey their passions. Do not yield your members to sin as instruments of wickedness, but yield yourselves to God as men who have been brought from death to life, and your members to God as instruments of righteousness. For sin will have no dominion over you, since you are not under law but under grace.
>
> (Romans 6:12-14)

In his physical humanity, Christ has restored the dignity and holiness of man's physical nature and, in spite of sin, has returned human sexuality to its former beauty.

Sexuality is a uniquely personal and precious gift given by God and intended by the Lord to be used only when it is integrated into the relationship of one person to another in the complete and lifelong mutual gift of man and woman in the Sacrament of Marriage. Christ places sexual activity within the covenant commitment of marriage, in which 'a man leaves his father and his mother and cleaves to his wife, and they become one flesh' (Genesis 2:24). In St Matthew's Gospel, Jesus says, 'Have you not read that he who made them from the beginning made them male and female, and said, "For this reason a man shall leave his father and mother and be joined to his wife, and the two shall become one"? So they are no longer two but one' (Matthew 19:4-6a).

The human body is designed so that man and woman can both make a total gift of themselves to each other and receive the total gift of the other. This is the only divinely ordered sexual meaning and orientation of human bodies, what Pope John Paul II called the nuptial meaning of the human body. Authentic human sexual activity is therefore between a man and a woman. Anything else is disordered in the sight of God. The human body speaks its own language. It speaks of sensual pleasure, it speaks powerfully of physical love and even more powerfully of ecstatic spiritual union. Sexual intercourse, a gift from God, is something sacred, not to be trivialised or reduced to the level of erotic recreation or worse. Sex outside of the marriage covenant falls short of God's plan for a truly human life.

Jesus willed to be born into the home of Joseph and Mary. Their virginal marriage was an icon and a celebration of the coming of the Kingdom. Jesus the Returning King, the Son of God, made of their home a new temple. Mary is the Ark of the New Covenant where 'The Word became flesh and dwelt among us' (John 1:14). So marriage is a holy state made so by the presence of our Lord Jesus Christ.

At Cana, Jesus honoured the young couple by His presence. He honours every man and woman who enters the sacred covenant of Christian marriage with His sacramental presence and with all the grace and help that is unique to the Sacrament of Marriage. On their wedding day when a young married couple turns from the altar to process down the aisle of the church, Jesus Christ is with them. Through His grace their married life, their physical sexual life, their fertility, their child-bearing, are made holy and pleasing in the eyes of the Father.

There is a most beautiful teaching on Christian marriage in Chapter 5 of the Letter to the Ephesians. Many people who read this passage make little effort to understand it:

> Be subject to one another out of reverence for Christ. Wives, be subject to your husbands, as to the Lord. For the husband is the head of the wife as Christ is the head of the Church, his body, and is himself its Saviour. As the Church is subject to Christ, so let wives also be subject in everything to their husbands. Husbands, love your wives, as Christ loved the Church and gave Himself up for Her, that He might sanctify Her, having cleansed her by the washing of water with the word, that he might present the Church to himself in splendour, without spot or wrinkle or any such thing,

I Will Come Myself

that she might be holy and without blemish. Even so husbands should love their wives as their own bodies. He who loves his wife loves himself. For no man ever hates his own flesh, but nourishes and cherishes it, as Christ does the Church, because we are members of His body. 'For this reason a man shall leave his father and mother and be joined to his wife, and the two shall become one flesh.' This is a great mystery, and I mean in reference to Christ and the Church; however, let each one of you love his wife as himself.

(Ephesians 5:21-33)

Nowhere in Sacred Scripture does it say that women should live in subjection to man; far from it. In the *Catechism of the Catholic Church* we read:

Man and woman have been *created*, which is to say, willed by God: on the one hand, in perfect equality as human persons; on the other, in their respective beings as man and woman. 'Being man' or 'being woman' is a reality which is good and willed by God: man and woman possess an inalienable dignity which comes to them immediately from God their Creator. Man and woman are both with one and the same dignity 'in the image of God'. In their 'being-man' and 'being-woman', they reflect the Creator's wisdom and goodness.

(*CCC*: 369)

But let me return to St Paul. 'Wives be subject to your husbands' ... if one stopped there, then there would be reason to complain. But the words 'as to the Lord' make all the difference. This is not subjection to male domination, but rather the freely given respect and submission of a loving spouse. Similarly, you can't just say that the husband is the 'head of the wife' and leave it at that. You have to add 'as Christ is head of the Church'. St Paul's understanding of subjection is one of the total reciprocal love between Christ and the Church. This is his icon for Christian marriage. Husbands, on the other hand, are given an even more serious injunction by St Paul. He says, 'Husbands, love your wives, as Christ loved the Church and gave himself up for her' (Ephesians 5:25). St Paul is teaching us to live out the true, traditional understanding of the respective roles of husband and wife. The wife is the heart of the family and the husband is the head. In many families that I have been privileged to know, I have noticed a great deal of mutual submissive agreement between husbands and wives. There is no confusion between them when they live out their separate roles guided by the Holy Spirit.

After my ordination I went home for my first visit in several years. At the request of my mother I went to visit my neighbours. One was an old Protestant man who had a wry sense of humor.

He said to me, 'You priests don't get married. Aren't you the lucky man?' And with a glint in his eye and a little smile he said, 'You know, when I was courting my wife, I loved her so much that I could've eaten her. Now fifty years later I'm sorry I didn't.' An old chestnut to be sure, but he was expressing a truth to a young and inexperienced celibate – namely, that marriage, like celibacy, requires a lot of self-giving.

It is because of the exalted nature of human sexuality that Jesus gave us his teaching on celibacy. In Matthew 19, Jesus speaks to His apostles about being eunuchs, that is being celibate 'for the sake of the kingdom of heaven' (Matthew 19:12). Here Jesus challenges His followers to live the life of the Kingdom of God here on earth. The answer to His call has manifested itself down the centuries in the lives of countless men and women who have dedicated themselves to live the evangelical counsels of poverty, chastity, and obedience. A person who embraces the celibate state according to the mind of Christ offers to God something noble and deeply personal to himself. Jesus does not call us to deny or to repress our sexuality, but rather to present it as a free gift, a love-offering to Him for the sake of the Gospel.

In his little book *Chastity*, Fr Raneiro Cantalamessa comments on how people wonder why Catholic priests have to be celibate. He maintains that the question ought to be not 'Why are Catholic priests called to be celibate?' but rather 'Why are not all ministers of the Gospel celibate?'

The world we live in today does not understand celibacy and often ridicules it, not understanding that it is another way in which the human person may live out his or her sexual existence. Chastity is for everyone – the truth is that no one can live a completely sexually free unrestrained lifestyle. This was never God's plan for human beings. Everyone must live the life of chastity – the married in being faithful to their spouses, and the celibate in fidelity to their vows. The vocation of single life also brings with it the call to chastity in faithfulness to the law of Christ. Jesus proclaimed, 'that every one who looks at a woman lustfully has already committed adultery with her in his heart' (Matthew 5:28).

In his sublime encyclical *Deus Caritas Est* Pope Benedict XVI writes:

> Man is truly himself when his body and soul are intimately united; the challenge of *eros* can be said to be truly overcome when this unification is achieved. Should he aspire to be pure spirit and to reject the flesh as pertaining to his animal nature alone, then spirit and body would both lose their dignity. On the other hand, should he deny the spirit and consider matter, the body, as the only reality, he would likewise lose his greatness. The epicure Gassendi used to offer Descartes the humorous greeting: 'O Soul!' And Descartes would reply: 'O Flesh!' Yet it is neither the spirit alone nor the body alone that loves: it is man, the person, a unified creature composed of body and soul, who loves. Only when both dimensions are truly united, does man attain his full stature. Only thus is love – *eros* – able to mature and attain its authentic grandeur.
>
> (*Deus Caritas Est*: 5)

Homosexuality is one of the most fraught moral issues of our time and there are many opinions about it.

I Will Come Myself

Normally people have the capacity for sexual activity, which is to be exercised only within the sanctity of the marriage covenant of man and woman as husband and wife. The gay movement's insistence that homosexuals have a right to be sexually active has made it difficult to have a meaningful dialogue about how to live with the homosexual orientation.

The Church teaching on homosexuality can be found in the *Catechism of the Catholic Church*:

> The number of men and women who have deep-seated homosexual tendencies is not negligible. This inclination, which is objectively disordered, constitutes for most of them a trial. They must be accepted with respect, compassion, and sensitivity. Every sign of unjust discrimination in their regard should be avoided. These persons are called to fulfill God's will in their lives and, if they are Christians, to unite to the sacrifice of the Lord's Cross the difficulties they may encounter from their condition. Homosexual persons are called to chastity. By the virtues of self-mastery that teach them inner freedom, at times by the support of disinterested friendship, by prayer and sacramental grace, they can and should gradually and resolutely approach Christian perfection.
>
> (*CCC*: 2358, 2359)

There are multitudes of men and women who never get married for one reason or another and who live chaste lives of purity, self-control and genuine holiness. Many such people find great fulfillment in serving others through social involvement or within the Church. Add to this the great army of priests and religious who for centuries have served God and the Church as celibates.

A priest once told me a story about two men who had lived together for many years. Every day they would go to work in different parts of the city. One day, each of them, without the other knowing it, was drawn to visit a nearby church. While there, each was convicted of the need to change his way of life. They came home and each shared with one another what had happened. They agreed to begin a new way of life and to return to God and the practice of their Catholic faith.

Over my years of priestly ministry, I have met many homosexual people, but I have never met one who experienced his or her sexual orientation as anything other than a heavy cross. By the same token, I know many who have come to terms with this burden, who live virtuous lives, and have arrived at great holiness.

Chapter 18
Christ or Caesar?

The beginning of the Irish Constitution invokes the Blessed Trinity, and the United States Declaration of Independence refers to God the Creator. The proposed Constitution for the European Union makes no mention of God or of the Church, even though history clearly shows that without the Church there would be no Europe as we now know it.

These last few decades have seen a great falling away from the Christian faith and the Catholic Church. People have been behaving as though God had not revealed Himself, as if there were no Commandments and no Gospel. Many have knowingly and quite deliberately turned their back on God and on the Church. They have used certain scandals in the Church as their excuse to abandon God and pay no heed to His revealed word or to His Son Jesus Christ. Well-educated people, who are careful and even-handed about matters relating to their careers and other things, bring none of this acumen to bear when it comes to faith and religion. They seem content to go along with the crowd and accept whatever is in vogue at the time. People have become ashamed of Jesus Christ and are embarrassed to call themselves Catholic. This displays a good deal of hypocrisy, intellectual dishonesty and moral cowardice.

In the Gospel, Jesus has words for people who profess one thing and do something else:

> Woe to you, scribes and Pharisees, hypocrites! because you shut the kingdom of heaven against men; for you neither enter yourselves, nor allow those who would enter to go in. Woe to you, scribes and Pharisees, hypocrites! for you traverse sea and land to make a single proselyte, and when he becomes a proselyte, you make him twice as much a child of hell as yourselves ... Woe to you, scribes and Pharisees, hypocrites! for you tithe mint and dill and cummin, and have neglected the weightier matters of the law, justice and mercy and faith; these you ought to have done, without neglecting the others. You blind guides, straining out a gnat and swallowing a camel.
>
> (Matthew 23:13-15/23-24)

For most of my priestly life I have been involved in ministering to priests. Because of this I am acutely aware of the pain and scandal that the criminal behaviour of some priests has caused to so many innocent people. Jesus speaks of this in the Gospel:

> Whoever receives one such child in My name receives Me; but whoever causes one

of these little ones who believe in Me to
sin, it would be better for him to have a
great mill stone fastened around his neck
and to be drowned in the depth of the sea.
(Matthew 18:5-6)

For any person to be guilty of sins against children is
bad enough, but for a priest to do so is unspeakable.
The spiritual shock, the emotional violation, the moral
scandal, the horrific memories can be understood only
by the victims themselves. The suffering which they
and their families must endure over a lifetime is beyond
our understanding. It is a veritable crucifixion. A
lifetime of prayer, penance and reparation is needed to
expiate such a sin. As a priest, I feel strongly obligated
to remember such innocent victims in prayer and
especially at the Holy Eucharist.

A prayer which I often say for them is the *Chaplet of
Divine Mercy*. This beautiful devotion contains a
perfect prayer of reparation.

Eternal Father, I offer You the Body and
Blood, Soul and Divinity of Your dearly
beloved Son, our Lord Jesus Christ, in
atonement for our sins and those of the
whole world.

Speaking for the vast army of good and virtuous priests,
I can say that many are hurt at being tarred with the
same brush as their unfortunate colleagues. Most
people see their priests going about the work of total
dedication to their people. A couple of years ago,
travelling in the United States, I had a very unusual

experience relating to this. While waiting at the gate before boarding a plane, I became aware of a young business man, with a briefcase, who was staring at me. This was during the time of the clerical scandals in a prominent diocese in the United States which were getting maximum publicity in the American media. I was afraid that this young man would come over at any moment and berate me just for being a priest. I resigned myself to whatever might or might not come. Eventually, just when we were called to board the plane, he walked over to me. What he did surprised me.

He came over to me, shook my hand and said, 'Father, I just want to thank you for being a priest. You know, I am a Catholic, and all that matters to me is my faith in Jesus Christ and my love for the Church. So, thank you again for being a priest.' At that he walked off.

The old saying, 'You can't scandalise saints or sinners,' is still true. The saints will always understand; the sinners won't care. Good people are always able to see beyond the sinful person, the vessel of clay. They know that the Church is the Body of Christ which, in spite of every kind of scandal, will never fail or be destroyed. As a priest, I may be a great sinner, but the power and holiness of the priesthood, which is the power and holiness of Jesus Christ the Eternal High Priest, never falters. The Word of God will always prevail and drive out all darkness.

The spiritual authority in the Church which Jesus imparted to Peter remains in the person of the Pope. The apostles and their successors, the bishops, went forth with the message of the Gospel, bringing it to the farthest corners of the earth. Since that time, God has

I Will Come Myself

continued to raise up great men and women, priests, religious and lay people, who have borne witness to the message of the Gospel all over the world performing wonderful works of evangelisation through the power of the Holy Spirit.

In spite of schisms and 'reformations', the integrity of Christ's message of salvation subsists in the Catholic Church. The Lord has never failed to raise up great men and women like St Patrick and St Thomas More, St Catherine of Sienna, St Theresa, St Francis, St Vincent de Paul, Blessed Teresa of Calcutta and Pope John Paul II. These saints and thousands like them performed great works in the Church and in the world – always faithful to the message of Christ, always in solidarity with the Church's teaching, always heroic in their obedience. They were people for whom their faith in Jesus Christ and their love for the Church meant everything.

In our own time we have lived through an age of disobedience. Many people have cast a cold, cynical eye on Christ and His message, and through ridicule and blasphemy, have inflicted deep wounds on the Church. Their denial of God's revelation is almost total and their lives and influence have created a dark world where it is difficult to live a dignified human life.

St Paul in his Letter to the Romans might well have been describing our own times when he wrote:

> For the wrath of God is revealed from heaven against all ungodliness and wickedness of men who by their wickedness suppress the truth. For what can be known about God is plain to them,

because God has shown it to them. Ever since the creation of the world his invisible nature, namely, his eternal power and deity, has been clearly perceived in the things that have been made. So they are without excuse; for although they knew God they did not honor him as God or give thanks to him, but they became futile in their thinking and their senseless minds were darkened. Claiming to be wise, they became fools, and exchanged the glory of the immortal God for images resembling mortal man or birds or animals or reptiles. Therefore God gave them up in the lusts of their hearts to impurity, to the dishonoring of their bodies among themselves, because they exchanged the truth about God for a lie and worshiped and served the creature rather than the Creator, who is blessed for ever! Amen. For this reason God gave them up to dishonorable passions. Their women exchanged natural relations for unnatural, and the men likewise gave up natural relations with women and were consumed with passion for one another, men committing shameless acts with men and receiving in their own persons the due penalty for their error. And since they did not see fit to acknowledge God, God gave them up to a base mind and to improper conduct. They were filled with all manner of wickedness, evil, covetousness, malice. Full of envy, murder, strife, deceit,

I Will Come Myself

malignity, they are gossips, slanderers, haters of God, insolent, haughty, boastful, inventors of evil, disobedient to parents, foolish, faithless, heartless, ruthless. Though they know God's decree that those who do such things deserve to die, they not only do them but approve those who practice them.

(Romans 1:18-32)

I have lived in a century that has seen two world wars and a dozen other wars. We have seen the demonic philosophies of Nazism and Communism bring ruination to the social and religious cultures of many nations. Men have again chosen to live apart from God's law and have created a world where the death of someone is often proposed as a solution to one problem or another, and where depraved human behaviour is thought of as normal and acceptable.

The reality is that some things that our elected representatives vote on pertain only indirectly to fundamental moral matters, while other things pertain directly to fundamental moral matters. People in government and elected representatives, if Christian, may not vote for abortion or euthanasia regardless of the pressure they may feel from their constituents. To do so inflicts great harm.

Pope John Paul II wrote two great encyclicals, *The Splendor of Truth* and *The Gospel of Life*, to remind the world that there are such things as eternal truth and moral norms, which never pass away and by which all men must live. The question then remains, who is going to guide us and what moral law is going to govern our lives? Will it be God's law or will it be the philosophy of a secular world, where moral relativism, violence, the culture of death and darkness prevail?

Chapter 19
Didn't That Go Out After Vatican II?

Friends of mine have a son who is a successful lawyer. This young man is a graduate from a famous Catholic college. He gave up the practice of his faith and is married outside of the Church. Invariably on the occasions I would meet him, he lectured me on 'what's wrong with the Catholic Church'. After several of these encounters, I eventually lost my patience; I could take it no longer.

I said to him, 'Let me tell you what's wrong with the Catholic Church. It is full of people like you who never go to Mass, don't bother to get married or have their children baptised, don't go to Confession, don't pray and have no concern for the poor or anybody else; who criticise priests, brothers, nuns and other dedicated folk. That is what I think is wrong with the Catholic Church.'

I felt like Jesus in the temple. I was mad at him and he knew it. That was the last time he lectured me on that topic.

This is the problem with many Catholics. They want the Church on their own terms and obedience is not part of their agenda. They want all the benefits of being

Catholic, but none of the obligations. They live on the periphery of the Church's life. They do not lead a sacramental life. They do not pray. They sometimes live very sinful lives. They are completely taken over by the world with its pride, greed, social ambition and the pleasures of drink and sex. Their lives are selfish and ego-centric. In a life completely centered on themselves they have no desire for God. But they will come to baptisms and weddings. They will even go up to receive Holy Communion. 'Why not? I am a Catholic, after all.'

The end product of this kind of lifestyle is a deep dissatisfaction. The fact is that we are made for God and the space in our hearts that is destined for Him can never be filled by *la dolce vita*. No jet-set lifestyle, no drugs, no alcohol, no sex, nor anything else can ever make us happy, or fill the void left by the absence of the living God.

St Augustine wrote his often-quoted words to express a reality from which no human being can escape:

> You are great, Lord, and worthy of our highest praise; Your power is great and there is no limit to Your wisdom. Man, a tiny part of your creation, wishes to praise you. Though he bears about him his mortality, the evidence of his sin and the evidence that you resist the proud, yet this man, a tiny part of your creation, wishes to praise you. It is you who move man to delight in your praise. For you have made us for yourself, and our heart is restless until it rests in you.
>
> (*Liturgy of the Hours.* Vol. III, p. 290)

I Will Come Myself

Ultimately such people can become so cut off from any form of contact with God's grace that they are not even aware of how sinful their lives have become. They are literally living in a state of mortal, lethal sinfulness. Their moral compass no longer works and slowly, but surely, they become so confused that darkness becomes light and evil becomes good. Satan is never far from such people, urging them on to ultimate destruction. But neither is God far off. 'His mercy endures forever' (Psalm 136).

Obviously, not everyone lives such dark and sinful lives. God calls everyone to a life of holiness and union with Himself, but unfortunately many become caught up in a life of compromise. They are lukewarm. Their aim in life is the same as that of so many people – the pursuit of wealth and social respectability. They are ruled by the opinions of others and various forms of *correctness*. They pray little. God is kept at a distance. They are on the runway and air traffic-control has given them clearance, but they never take off.

Once some people asked me about the themes of the mission I was giving. When I told them that our first evening was devoted to the theme of repentance and the Sacrament of Reconciliation, one of them said, 'You know, I haven't been to Confession for twenty years. I thought all that went out after Vatican II.'

There are many Catholics who somehow have the impression that the Sacrament of Reconciliation is no longer necessary in the practice of our Catholic faith. Not so. Truth to tell, there is a very great need for the Church in our time to call people to repent of their sins in this merciful encounter with the risen, forgiving Christ, the Sacrament of Reconciliation.

Another unfortunate attitude regarding this sacrament I describe as the 'carwash mentality'. Far too many people think that Confession is all that is required and there is no real need for amendment of life. Receiving the Sacrament of Reconciliation presumes a desire to be converted and to change one's life.

Some years ago I was celebrating Mass at a huge conference in Asia. The auditorium was filled with about two thousand people. In the procession on my way to celebrate the Eucharist, a man approached me and asked me if I could hear his Confession. I said, 'No, I cannot. I must go to celebrate Mass.' As I walked away from him I heard a voice say to me, 'Go back and hear his Confession.' I immediately turned around and went back, took him aside and heard his Confession. I was told afterwards that this man had an extraordinary experience of the merciful forgiving Christ which apparently transformed his whole life. As a priest I have witnessed many such graces through the Sacrament of Reconciliation and on that day I made a resolution that I will always hear the Confession of anyone who asks me, no matter how much I might be pressed for time.

People should not be afraid to look their sins and demons in the face. God gives us the Commandments, and the Church teaches us and helps us to form our conscience. Sin doesn't change that much; it just puts on a new face.

Chapter 20
Prayer

In July of 1985 I first visited Medjugorje, a small village in Bosnia-Hercegovina where our Blessed Lady was said to be appearing. Before going, I had watched a video made by an English priest in which he spoke of his visit to Medjugorje and how he had received a personal message from our Blessed Lady.

When I got there I was preoccupied and distracted, wondering what it might be like to receive a personal message from the Mother of God. The more I tried to put it out of my mind, the more it seemed to haunt me. So, I talked to Sr Janja about it. Sr Janja Boras is a wonderful Franciscan sister who worked in Medjugorje during the early years of the apparitions of Our Lady. She had worked in the United States for some years and was one of the few people in Medjugorje who could speak English. She was a great help to me and many others who went there. I talked to Sr Janja about the possibility of receiving a personal message from our Blessed Lady. She said, 'Go away and pray and fast and ask the Lord, and come back and see me tomorrow.'

The next day before I had a chance to speak to her, Sr Janja said, 'Father, you should ask our Blessed

Mother, since you seem to be at a crossroads in your ministry at this time.'

'How would I go about that?' I asked her.

'Well,' she said, 'Write out your questions and I will pass them on to Marija, the visionary, and she will ask the Gospa (their name for Our Lady).'

After much prayer I wrote out my questions and, as it turned out, I was in the room of the apparitions that evening and saw Marija holding my piece of paper in her hand. I could hardly wait to ask Marija what the Gospa had to say to me. She smiled and said, 'Well, Father, you saw me there with your written note in my hand.'

'Yes, Marija,' I said, 'What did she say?'

She replied, 'Father, I said to the Gospa, "There is a priest here who wants to ask you these questions. What do you have to say to him?"'

Marija continued, 'The Gospa smiled and said, "Tell him that all his questions will be answered in prayer."'

I was taken aback by this answer and said to Marija, 'Is that all she said?'

'Yes,' said Marija, '"Tell him all his questions will be answered in prayer."'

I went away disappointed. Somehow the response of the Gospa was not what I was expecting. It was not until I began to ponder this message that I came to realise that if it did not come from the Mother of God, it was a message worthy of her. It did not pander to my spiritual curiosity, but instead challenged me with the great truth and the importance of believing that every prayer we make to God will be heard and heeded. These words have remained with me ever since and they challenge me every day of my life. They have been a rock of truth for me.

Cardinal Ratzinger, before he became Pope Benedict XVI, wrote this about prayer: 'Prayer is hope in action; prayer is the language of hope. We pray and hope for what can only be given to us.'

After many years in the priestly ministry I have come to realise the truth of this. Everything I do as a priest is given to me as a gift from the Lord, whether it is celebrating the sacraments, preaching the Word of God, ministering to the poor and desolate, or listening to the sufferings of afflicted people. Everything that I need as a priest comes to me from God and that is why I must be in constant prayer with Him.

Prayer is the highest form of theology, as St Thomas Aquinas reminded us when he said, 'I learned more at the foot of the crucifix than in all my studies.'

Unfortunately, there are many who prefer to go their own way without any reference to God or His providence. They never pray. They plan their lives, their careers, their family, their future, as if God did not exist.

We must never forget that our God, the One who Jesus describes in the Gospel, is a loving and caring Father. He made in His own image and likeness, and made us free. That mankind betrayed this freedom and fell from original justice is not God's fault. After the fall, God in His love immediately restored us once more and justified and redeemed us in the blood of His beloved Son shed for us on the Cross. Our God is not out to get us or turn our lives into some kind of miserable bondage. He is not a fearful, vengeful judge. He is a loving, understanding, forgiving Father who wants us to be happy. And He knows that His children can only be happy with Him.

Some people imagine that if they pray and draw near to God, He will make their lives miserable and so they purposely avoid prayer. The devil is never far away when we are having these kinds of thoughts, encouraging us to keep our distance from God. People instead tell themselves, this person will make me happy; or this money will make me happy; or if I get this, I wouldn't want anything else.

God our Father desires us to believe in His love for us. Jesus our Lord wants us to trust in Him for everything. He said in the Gospel, 'Ask, and it will be given you; seek, and you will find; knock, and it will be will be opened to you' (Luke 11:9).

We should pray with a living faith. Sometimes people think to themselves, I knew before I prayed that I wouldn't get it. Instead they should say, 'Lord, I know You are going to grant my prayer, and if You don't, it will only be because You want to give me something better than what I am asking.' God loves faith like this.

God will not do magic tricks for us. In teaching us the Our Father, He instructs us to ask for our daily bread. That is to say, we should ask for the things we need in life, like a good job and enough to provide for one's family. Saying formal prayers is good, but having a conversation with God can be more real, both for ourselves and for the Lord. For instance, in praying for someone at work, you could simply say to Jesus, 'Lord Jesus, my boss is driving me insane. I cannot stand it any longer. I don't want to be like this, so Lord, You've got to help me to be patient and forgiving and loving.' Or, 'Lord, this person has wounded me deeply for years and I have not been able to forgive. Help me, Father, to let go of this. Help me to forgive. Empty out this reservoir of pain and resentment and fill me with the love of Your own heart.'

If we take God seriously as our loving Father, and Jesus as our Brother, then we can ask for whatever we need and it will be given to us. My friend Joe once said a beautiful thing to me, 'You know, Father, all I have ever wanted out of life God has already given me – my beautiful wife Jackie, my children – Mary, Clare, Michael, Dominic, Bernadette, Josephine and Faustina. God has richly blessed me. He has given me everything I have asked Him and I could never thank Him enough.'

No one in the Old Testament ever dared to call God 'Father' or even utter the name of God. Jesus was the first to do this. When the disciples asked Him, 'Lord, teach us to pray,' He said, 'When you pray, say, "Father, hallowed be thy name. Thy kingdom come. Give us each day our daily bread; and forgive us our sins, for we ourselves forgive every one who is indebted to us; and lead us not into temptation"' (Luke 11:1-4).

Commenting on this prayer of Jesus, St Ambrose wrote:

> O man, you did not dare to raise your face to heaven, you lowered your eyes to the earth, and suddenly you have received the grace of Christ; all your sins have been forgiven. From being a wicked servant you have become a good son ... Then raise your eyes to the Father who has begotten you through Baptism, to the Father who

has redeemed you through his Son, and say: 'Our Father ...' But do not claim any privilege. He is the Father in a special way only of Christ, but he is the common Father of us all, because while he has begotten only Christ, he has created us. Then also say by his grace, 'Our Father', so that you may merit being his son.

(St Ambrose, *De Sacr.*) (*CCC*: 2783)

Everyone at times experiences dryness and distraction when they try to pray. In these moments we need to call on the help of the Holy Spirit, who, as St Paul tells us, prays with us and in us: 'Likewise the Spirit helps us in our weakness; for we do not know how to pray as we ought, but the Spirit Himself intercedes for us with sighs too deep for words. And He who searches the hearts of man knows what is the mind of the Spirit, because the Spirit intercedes for the saints according to the will of God' (Romans 8:26-27).

For those whose spiritual dryness brings them to the edge of hopeless despair, Pope Benedict has a word of consolation in his encyclical on hope.

A first essential setting for learning hope is prayer. When no one listens to me any more, God still listens to me. When I can no longer talk to anyone or call upon anyone, I can always talk to God. When there is no longer anyone to help me deal with a need or expectation that goes beyond the human capacity for hope, he can help me. When I have been plunged

I Will Come Myself

into complete solitude ... if I pray I am never totally alone.

(Spe Salvi: 32)

One great form of Christian prayer has its origin in the spirituality of the Eastern Church. It is called The Jesus Prayer: 'Lord Jesus Christ, Son of God, be merciful to me, a sinner.' The idea is to pray this prayer over and over until it begins to echo in our soul after we have ceased saying it with our lips. This kind of prayer stills the body, soul and spirit, and helps us to be in the presence of God. This prayer is rooted in Scripture.

> He also told this parable to some who trusted in themselves that they were righteous and despised others: 'Two men went up into the temple to pray, one a Pharisee and the other a tax collector. The Pharisee stood and prayed thus with himself, "God, I thank thee that I am not like other men, extortioners, unjust, adulterers, or even like this tax collector. I fast twice a week, I give tithes of all that I get." But the tax collector, standing far off, would not even lift up his eyes to heaven, but beat his breast, saying, "God, be merciful to me a sinner!" I tell you, this man went down to his house justified rather than the other; for every one who exalts himself will be humbled, but he who humbles himself will be exalted.'
>
> (Luke 18:9-14)

Our Blessed Mother has her own school of prayer. It is called the Rosary. In this prayer, Mary invites us, through the repetition of the Hail Mary, to contemplate Jesus, her Son, in His life and mysteries. It is a prayer of extraordinary worth and effectiveness. It is a fast track to the contemplative life and a strong protection against the forces of evil.

Wouldn't it be great to see the practice of the family Rosary restored again to Catholic homes? It would heal and transform family life. The Rosary has proved to be a deep well-spring of holiness for generations of Mary's children. Those who say the Rosary is nothing but a monotonous repetition of Hail Marys show a poor understanding of this most powerful prayer.

St Pio of Pietrelcina (Padre Pio) said that the Rosary is like a giant sword which Mary our Mother places in the hands of her children to defend themselves against the attacks of the devil. I have met many people who have told me just that. Like myself, they had experienced moments of intense spiritual warfare in which the Rosary proved to be a powerfully effective weapon against the enemy. Mary always crushes the head of the serpent.

Chapter 21
Mary and Her Children

The Lord God said to the serpent, '... I will put enmity between you and the woman, and between your seed and her seed; he will bruise your head, and you shall bruise his heel'.

(Genesis 3:14-15)

In the early 1980s I met an American Daughter of Charity of St Vincent de Paul named Sr Zoe. She asked me whether women's lib had reached Ireland yet.

I said, 'I don't think so.' I was wrong. Of course it had indeed reached Ireland and was alive and well and growing fast.

'Well,' said Sr Zoe, 'if it hasn't, it soon will.'

Sr Zoe had obtained a doctorate degree in Church history and was teaching in a seminary in the United States. She said, 'You know, there are many issues concerning women in the Church which need to be addressed and regarding some, the women's movement has much good to say. But as for the rest of their ideas, they tend to be anti-Christian and anti-Church.'

She went on to say, 'History has shown that whenever anything was going wrong with the Church or with society, it could always be traced back to what was going wrong with women.'

I never did get a chance to ask her what she meant by that, but the intervening years have confirmed the truth of what she said. *Women's lib* has long since transmuted into secular feminism which, aided and abetted by the media with their strong liberal secularist agenda, has become an enemy of God and the Church. Politicians too have been instrumental in promoting the secular feminist agenda. In most political parties, it is difficult to find anyone who is willing to stand up and be counted, especially when it comes to issues concerning life and the family. Every year in Washington there is a pro-life march with a rally on the mall in front of the Houses of Congress. Before this rally, the pro-abortion groups have their meeting in the auditorium of a Washington hotel. While the pro-abortion rally is attended by many high-profiled politicians, very few attend the pro-life rally.

As for issues such as *Natural Family Planning,* feminists maintain a stony silence, as unfortunately do many Catholics. It is surprising how little this important development of *Natural Family Planning* is spoken of. I suppose it is because it does not provide the instant solution to the 'fertility problem' insisted on by a modern society. The pill is easy and trendy, even though it drags women down and debases their womanhood and their femininity by portraying fertility as though it were a curse or some awful malady needing to be cured.

How often the proposed solution to so many of the problems of the underdeveloped world is to kill

I Will Come Myself

someone. Almost always, world banking organisations tie their loans of money to an insistence that the receiving governments put in place programs of sterilisation, contraception and abortion. The poor do not have much in this world, but they do have the comfort and richness of their children. The grey-suited men (women) should be reminded that there are no unwanted children. God who created them wants them all. It is up to the super-affluent world to help them out of their oppression and misery, and not to immerse them deeper into it. This indeed is the unacceptable face of capitalism. Bishop Helder Camara spoke the famous words, 'When I feed the poor, they call me a saint; but when I ask why the poor are hungry, they call me a Communist.'

It is into this bleak, neo-pagan world that the light of the Holy Spirit has shone again in the person of Mary, the Immaculate Mother of our Saviour. For some years now we have been witnessing a widespread renewal of awareness of the person of Mary and her place in the world. The Spirit is pointing the attention of the Church and the world to Mary. This awareness was given great impetus by Pope John Paul II who was never ashamed to proclaim himself a child of his mother. Even in his motto, *Totus Tuus*, he declared his complete dedication to our heavenly mother, 'I am all yours, Mary, and all that I have is yours.'

Mary is pre-eminently a woman of the Bible. She is the bridge over which we cross from the Old Testament to the New. She is the promised woman of Genesis. She is the New Eve whose obedience undid the harm wrought by our first parents. Did every Jewish girl have a golden dream in which she imagined that she might be chosen to be the Mother of the Messiah King? Did Mary have such a dream? We read in the Gospel of Luke:

> In the sixth month the angel Gabriel was sent from God to a city of Galilee named Nazareth, to a virgin betrothed to a man whose name was Joseph, of the house of David; and the virgin's name was Mary. And he came to her and said, 'Hail, full of grace, the Lord is with you!' But she was greatly troubled at the saying, and considered in her mind what sort of greeting this might be. And the angel said to her, 'Do not be afraid, Mary, for you have found favour with God. And behold, you will conceive in your womb and bear a son, and you shall call his name Jesus. He will be great, and will be called the Son of the Most High; and the Lord God will give to him the throne of his father David, and he will reign over the house of Jacob for ever; and of his kingdom there will be no end.' And Mary said to the angel, 'How can this be, since I have no husband?' And the angel said to her, 'The Holy Spirit will come upon you, and the power of the Most High will overshadow you; therefore the child to be born will be called holy, the Son of God. And behold, your kinswoman Elizabeth in her old age has also conceived a son; and this is the sixth month with her who was called barren. For with God

I Will Come Myself

nothing will be impossible.' And Mary said,
'Behold, I am the handmaid of the Lord;
let it be to me according to your word.'
And the angel departed from her.

(Luke 1:26-38)

The Lord had prepared Mary's spirit for this message of the angel Gabriel. She had been immaculately conceived in her mother's womb, which meant that no trace of Original Sin or any other sin was ever found in her. Nothing clouded her intellect and nothing disordered would affect her will. Her dialogue with the angel was brief; her consent was swift and sure. 'Be it done unto me according to thy word.' Mercifully, Joseph, too, had his annunciation and then took Mary into his home where they began, literally, to live the life of the Heavenly Kingdom in the presence of the Word made flesh, the Son of the Living God. It is hard for us to imagine the kind of interior life that Mary enjoyed. Her relationship to the Blessed Trinity was unique beyond all telling.

Mary is ever a mortal human being and yet she is drawn as near to divinity as it is possible to come. The very life of God comes to dwell within her flesh and blood. Mary lived in Nazareth with her Son and her husband, doing all the things that a wife and mother did in her day – things relating to food, clothing, housekeeping, living in a village community. I once saw a carving of Mary dressed as a peasant woman, a water jar in the crook of her left arm and holding the hand of the boy Jesus in her right hand. I have often mused on what the local women thought of Mary and what they might have said about her: 'Do you know Mary, the wife of Joseph the carpenter? Isn't she special? What is it about her anyway? And that little Boy of hers?'

There was little of human life that was alien to Mary of Nazareth. Like everyone else in the village, she was a fairly poor person struggling to make ends meet. Little did her neighbours know that this young woman was the Mother of God and the Queen of the Universe, and that her 'little Boy' was the promised Messiah who would grow up and accomplish our redemption and our deliverance from sin and eternal death.

God is always involved in Mary's life, speaking to her, directing her, guiding her, and protecting her and her Child from harm. After her return to Nazareth, she continues to ponder everything in her heart. She watches her Son grow into boyhood, adolescence and manhood. Never for a moment is she unaware of who her Son is and who she herself is. She is the Mother of Jesus and Jesus is her Son. She knows Him in every facet of His divine humanity. St Luke sums it up in a few words: 'And he went down with them and came to Nazareth, and was obedient to them; and his mother kept all of these things in her heart' (Luke 2:51).

In the hidden life Mary teaches us how we too must live. Even though she knows that Jesus is the Messiah, she does not know all of God's plan. Mary, like us, must walk in faith in a life lived day by day, week by week, year by year.

At the marriage feast of Cana, Jesus was there with His disciples when the wine runs out, and Mary, to forestall the impending embarrassment to their host, whispers to Jesus, 'They have no wine.'

Jesus says, 'Woman, what have you to do with me? My hour has not yet come' (John 2:4). Mary was not sure what Jesus was going to do, but she believed that He would do something and that it would be the best and most perfect thing. So she instructed the chief steward, 'Do whatever He tells you' (John 2:5). At that moment we witness a change in Mary's relationship with Jesus. He remains her Son, but now she must relate to Him as her Messiah and her Saviour.

We witness at Cana the beginning of the new motherhood which Jesus has destined for Mary. He leads her from merely biological motherhood to becoming the mother of all the faithful. During their hidden life together Mary is perceived to be the mother of the physical body of Jesus. From now on Jesus prepares her for the new motherhood of His Mystical Body, the Church.

In the Gospel of John we observe a further transformation of Mary's role on Calvary:

> But standing by the cross of Jesus were his mother, and his mother's sister, Mary the wife of Clopas, and Mary Magdalene. When Jesus saw his mother, and the disciple whom he loved standing near, he said to his mother, 'Woman, behold your son!' Then he said to the disciple, 'Behold your mother!' And from that hour the disciple took her to his own home.
>
> (John 19:25-27)

Jesus from the Cross looks down at His mother and declares her to be the Mother of His Mystical Body, the Church, 'Woman, behold your son.' And we, children of our Heavenly Father, are entrusted to Mary as her children, 'Behold your mother.'

This transition to universal motherhood is completed in the Upper Room on the day of Pentecost. Mary is there with the disciples and the holy women when the Holy Spirit comes upon the disciples in the form of tongues of fire and they are filled with a boldness which drives them out from their hiding place, literally to the ends of the earth. Some of the Fathers of the Church and many saints have contemplated Mary as she sits among the apostles. They say that just as in Bethlehem Mary brought forth the physical body of Jesus, so now in the Upper Room she brings forth from her mystical womb the new Body of Jesus, the Church, which is made up of all the baptised. Mary, the Mother of Jesus, is now the mother of us all.

In His public ministry, Jesus never lifts the veil of anonymity from His mother, even though there were opportunities to do so. I always smile when I read about the little woman as she listens to Jesus. She can think only of His mother. Unable to contain herself, she cries out, 'Blessed is the womb that bore you and the breasts that fed you' (Luke 11:27).

If she had been a little Dublin woman, she would have said, 'God bless You, Son. Your mother must have been a wonderful woman.' But Jesus does not take this opportunity to speak of His mother. He simply says, 'Blessed are those who hear the word of God and keep it.'

When her time on earth is over, Jesus lifts the veil of secrecy from His mother. Mary is taken bodily into Heaven and is proclaimed Queen of the Universe, Queen of Heaven and Queen of All Saints. A French priest wrote a book describing the creation of woman as the high point of God's creative work. He maintained that God created woman to be what he called the mediatrix of love, the open channel of love to all God's children and to the whole world. Satan, seeing what this would mean for humankind, came and offered Eve knowledge and power in exchange for this gift of God, and Eve believed him. But the Lord in his mercy immediately restored woman to her role of mediating His love in his promise of the New Eve, Mary, the Mother of Jesus.

Everywhere you look you see women channelling God's love – in their care for their children, for the sick, for poor people on the streets of Calcutta or in famine camps of Africa, in the hospitals of the world or the homes of the poor. Always there is a woman mediating the love of Christ. Mary does this for the whole world. She is the mother of the poor and of the rich. She listens to the cries of all her children in this valley of tears. She is the help of Christians, refuge of sinners and the comforter of the afflicted.

As a young priest, I was chaplain to those wonderful apostles of Our Lady, the Legion of Mary. Apart from their apostolic zeal, I have always been impressed by the amazing growth in holiness of those who joined the Legion of Mary. I have also observed this with other Marian groups. It seems that once they place themselves under the spiritual influence of the Blessed Virgin, they quickly become transformed by divine grace.

Going back to my short missionary career in Nigeria, I recall going to preach a retreat in a rural parish. Shortly after my arrival, a large delegation of young girls came to call at the house where I was lodging. They were all dressed in blue with white head scarves.

'Who are you?' I asked.

They replied, 'We are the Legion of Mary and we have come to help you during this retreat.'

'How can you help me?' I inquired.

'Well, Father,' they said, 'there is a lot of paganism in this place and nearly every house has some ju-ju from the local witch doctor.'

'Yes,' I said, 'but what can you do about that?'

They said, 'we can persuade the people to throw these things out of their homes and we will gather them up and burn them all at the end of the mission. But first, you must bless us with holy water and send us out. And you must bless our statue of Mary and the basin for collecting these pagan things.'

I was amazed that such young women were not afraid to do this, such was the confidence they had in the protection of their Blessed Mother. When I had completed these blessings I followed them as they marched down into the village in rows of four, 'like an army set in battle array'. They went around to each offending compound and stood there chanting songs like 'Mary is the Mother of Jesus, Mary Has Crushed the Serpent's Head' and other hymns and songs that they knew well. These holy young women lived under Mary's mantle and they knew that no evil could harm them. This is what the Mother of God does for all those who are childlike enough to come to her.

Today the Holy Spirit turns our gaze towards this 'woman clothed with the sun'.

> And a great portent appeared in heaven, a woman clothed with the sun, with the moon under her feet, and on her head a

crown of twelve stars; she was with child and she cried out in the pangs of birth, in anguish for delivery. And another portent appeared in Heaven; behold, a great red dragon, with seven heads and ten horns, and seven diadems upon his heads. His tail swept down a third of the stars of heaven, and cast them to the earth. And the dragon stood before the woman who was about to bear a child, that he might devour her child when she brought it forth; she brought forth a male child, one who is to rule all the nations with a rod of iron, but her child was caught up to God and to his throne, and the woman fled into the wilderness, where she has a place prepared by God.

(Revelation 12:1-6a)

Mary loves her children to come to her and ask her for the things they need. She loves us to pray her Rosary because it invites us to contemplate her Son as we pray each of the mysteries. She loves us to wear the Miraculous Medal or the brown Scapular and to crown her statues with flowers and light candles in her honour. Most of all, though, she loves us to live as she lived, to enter into the plan that God has for our lives. She wants us to turn away from sin and obey her Son by obeying the Church. She wants us to honour her by purity and virginity, by being true to the vows of our marriage, by living lives of holiness, prayer and self-sacrifice. She wants us more than all else to love and honour Jesus by a holy and blameless life.

I will finish this work with the beautiful words of Pope Benedict XVI which he addresses to Mary, Star of Hope:

> Through you, through your 'yes', the hope of the ages became reality, entering this world and its history. You bowed low before the greatness of this task and gave your consent: 'Behold, I am the handmaid of the Lord; let it be to me according to your word' (Luke 1:38). When you hastened with holy joy across the mountains of Judea to see your cousin Elizabeth, you became the image of the Church to come, which carries the hope of the world in her womb across the mountains of history. But alongside the joy which, with your Magnificat, you proclaimed in word and song for all the centuries to hear, you also knew the dark sayings of the prophets about the suffering of the servant of God in this world ... you saw the growing power of hostility and rejection which built up around Jesus until the hour of the Cross, when you had to look upon the Saviour of the world, the heir of David, the Son of God dying like a failure, exposed to mockery, between criminals. Then you received the word of Jesus: 'Woman, behold, your Son!' (John 19:26). From the Cross you received a new mission. From the Cross you became a mother in a new way: the mother of all

those who believe in your Son Jesus and wish to follow him.

(*Spe Salvi*: 50)

Mary is the promised woman of the Old Testament. She enters the history of salvation as the one chosen by God to be the mother of our Saviour Jesus Christ. Through her, Jesus speaks to a world waiting to be delivered from sin: '*I will come Myself* [and cure him]' (Matthew 8:7). Mary draws us closer to her Son. The last words she speaks in the Gospels are, in effect, her final words: 'Do whatever He tells you' (John 2:5). And so, Mary not only brought Christ to the world of the past, she teaches us the way we must go in the present if we are to experience the power of the Risen Christ.

Epilogue

When I had completed writing this book, I had no idea what title to give it. One morning while praying to Our Lady I mentioned my problem. Immediately the phrase from Matthew 8:7 *'I will come Myself'* dropped into my mind. I looked up various translations of this verse and all of them read *'I will come and heal him.'* It was only when I opened the Jerusalem Bible that I found, *'I will come Myself and heal him.'* As often as I have read these words I never gave much thought to their meaning. Reflecting on them now, however, I realise that they sum up the entire history of salvation from Genesis 3:15 to Revelations 22:20. For me, as a priest, these four words have taken on a powerful new meaning. During the course of my life I have witnessed how Christ Himself does come. These words describe every facet of the Christian life and the priestly ministry.

Perennially Jesus says, *I will come Myself* and make a home for you in My word and feed you on My Body and Blood and take away your sins and envelope you in My mercy. *I will come Myself* and dwell with you in marriage and teach you by My Holy Spirit and minister to you through My priests. *I will come Myself* and speak with you in prayer and visit you in the guise of the poor and needy. *I will come Myself* in the tender love of My Blessed Mother.

I have been a priest for many years and I have witnessed Christ's coming in all of these ways. Jesus Christ is risen. He is alive. He is real. He comes to us all, especially through the ministry of His priests.